HOW TO BECOME
DEAD RICH
—
HOWARD HODGSON

To

Dead

" I signed it anyway "

love

PAVILION

TO CHARLES

First published in Great Britain in 1992 by
PAVILION BOOKS LIMITED
196 Shaftesbury Avenue, London WC2H 8JL

Text copyright © 1992 Howard Hodgson
Foreword copyright © 1992 John Jay

Designed by Nigel Partridge

A CIP record for this book is available from the British Library.

ISBN 1 85145 855 2
10 9 8 7 6 5 4 3 2 1

Printed and bound in England at the Bath Press

CONTENTS

ACKNOWLEDGEMENTS

Let me thank Richard Branson, Chris Callaway, Rick Cressman, John Gunn, David Hancock, Gerald Ratner and Sir Michael Richardson for their assistance which was freely given. John Jay for writing the foreword and insisting that I should be brave enough to take on the House of Fraser in 1987. Hunter Davies for having the idea. Peter Pugh for the same and researching and collating the social and political pieces of the periods referred to. And my sons who waited patiently on many occasions in the Gulf of St Tropez for me to go sailing as I sat and scribbled away on the balcony of our home. Well done, boys – if we make the bestseller list the beers are on me.

I am grateful to the following for permission to quote from their works: the *Birmingham Post*, the *Financial Times*, the *Guardian*, the *Independent*, the *Investors Chronicle*, Kenneth Morgan *The People's Peace* OUP, the *New Statesman*, Martin Rowson, Sam Smith, John Taylor, Times Newspapers Ltd, USM Magazine, Philip Whitehead (*The Writing on the Wall*), and Andrew Yeo. Every effort has been made to trace the holders of copyright material. I apologise for any omissions in this respect and on notification undertake to make the appropriate acknowledgement in subsequent editions.

H.H.

FOREWORD

BY JOHN JAY

I first met Howard Hodgson over lunch at the Waldorf Hotel in the Aldwych in May 1986. His public relations consultant, Simon Preston, had called me to ask me if I was interested in an exclusive story on the forthcoming flotation of a funeral directing business.

The idea of a stock-market-quoted undertaker was unusual. But I had some knowledge of undertaking having covered a takeover battle involving one of Howard's competitors, Ingall's. The company had been the subject of a hostile bid from a regional cooperative society and the defending merchant bank, County, had come up with what it indelicately called 'the stiffs ratio'.

The proposition was that undertakers changed hands on the basis of an amount per funeral per year. At the time this was £1,000 said County to prove how mean the Co-op was being to Ingall's shareholders and I duly printed it. The result was an anguished letter from another of Howard's competitors, Great Southern, saying my 'stiffs ratio' was all wrong. The price per funeral was much lower.

The tone of the letter suggested my £1,000 had not gone down well at all – perhaps because Great Southern itself was in the midst of buying a rival and had been forced to raise its price. In fact I was right: the Co-op was seen off by a much higher bid from House of Fraser, which besides Harrods owned some Scottish undertakers.

So I came to that Waldorf lunch table with some knowledge about undertaking. But nothing could have prepared me for Howard. Instead of being confronted by some dark-suited, deeply sombre elderly gent, I came face to face with a casual, fresh-faced, longhaired young man who would have looked more at home on a tennis court than in a funeral cortège. The suit was razor sharp, the shirt came complete with a pin holding the collar together beneath the tie knot. This had been the fashion in the sixties, but had long died out in London although Howard still clung to it.

It was clear from the start he was no ordinary Unlisted Securities Market entrepreneur, that breed of the 1980s which became one of the leitmotifs of Thatcherism, and it became clearer still at the end of the lunch when I asked him for a photograph. Instead of a staid picture of a serious-looking man in a serious-looking suit, Preston tossed across the table a family snap of a beaming Howard in open shirt and pullover.

That Sunday I played Howard's eccentricity for all it was worth. Below this photo my introductory paragraph read as follows: 'Howard Hodgson does not look like a funeral director. But looks can deceive, for 36-year-old Hodgson is the chairman of a Birmingham funeral company that has been run by five generations of Hodgsons and was founded in 1850. Now the business, Hodgson Holdings, is being groomed for an Unlisted Securities Market flotation. . . .'

But though he was eccentric, Howard was also a classic Thatcherite businessman. He had picked his company up from his father for a mere £14,000 at a time when it was just hours from receivership. He had built it up through takeovers, rationalization and the introduction of rigorous efficiencies into one of the leading players in his industry.

And once on the stock-market, he marshalled the capital of the City of London to expand it much further still with a further blitz of takeovers. It was textbook stuff and it was hardly surprising that he quickly earned the soubriquet, 'The Lord Hanson of the funeral industry'. He deserved it.

Five years on, Hodgson is in semi-retirement, having built up the sort of wealth which should, if appropriately invested, keep his family in riches for generations. Yet at 41, he has lost none of his energy and is determined with his current businesses in financial services and business consultancy to build himself a second fortune. Not many entrepreneurs who sell up in the 40s achieve this but he has certainly got off to a cracking start.

A generation ago it looked as if the old formula of clogs to clogs in three generations might have applied to the Hodgsons except the path from poverty to wealth and back to poverty had taken four not three. But Howard has taken his family back to the top of the tree and his story should make fascinating reading for any entrepreneur who begins with nothing but an ambition to 'go for it' and transform his life.

It should also fascinate late-starters in life, people who find themselves 'coming from behind' and spend their early adult years trying desperately to catch up. Howard was lazy and unmotivated at school, achieved few academic qualifications, appears to have lived the life of a hippy for much of his late teens, but at 22 he suddenly woke up to what life was all about and focussed all his energies on the relentless pursuit of growth in his chosen business sector. For the rest, read on. . . .

JOHN JAY

INTRODUCTION

The original inspiration for this book was a desire to research a business in the Thatcher age. Had the rules been changed? Were businessmen, previously stifled, suddenly able to build large companies virtually from scratch and create riches for themselves and others? Were the reforms introduced by the Thatcher government essential for business to thrive?

I have catalogued the stages a business goes through as it grows from birth to comparative maturity and have used my own experience through each stage as an example. Moreover I have attempted to recall the prevailing social, economic and political cultures and fashions of the relevant period as such external forces have a great effect, if not on how you think, then on the decisions a businessman must take while prospering.

I admire objectivity greatly. I have tried to make this book objective. However if you get the impression that behind the objectivity there is strong support for Hodgson Holdings and me then you're probably right.

There are no prescribed rules of exactly how an individual can start a new enterprise and build it into an empire and in so doing become extremely wealthy. Indeed when I look back there have been many occasions in my experience when the only real difference between success and failure has been the courage that comes from inner motivation. Therefore with this book I have listed the essential ingredients you must have to start and build a successful business and I have included a few pointers towards the dos and don'ts that I have picked up along the way and have explained what it feels like as you progress down the road from a small business to a fully listed quoted company and, ultimately, financial wealth.

Undoubtedly, life in Britain for many, and especially for those in business, was different at the end of the 1980s from life at the end of the 1970s. At the end of the 1970s, Britain, and indeed other parts of the Western world, had suffered a decade – one could argue, in the case of Britain, anyway, several decades – of slow economic growth, weak management, and myopic trade unionism, restrictive practices throughout every part of society and debilitating inflation. Businessmen were demoralized, and it showed in the poor performance of companies and the economy generally. The stock-market, over a period of time a fair judge, valued British companies no more highly than it had done at the end of the 1960s. In fact, in view of the high inflation of that decade, in real terms it thought they were worth about a third as much. Inflation itself had been one of the most destabilizing elements of British society and British business. We live with inflation now as though it is inevitable. But it is not inevitable. For a long period the value of money remained stable. In 1910 the pound sterling bought pretty well what it had bought two and a half centuries before in 1660. Only in times of war when governments printed money had the pound depreciated. Indeed, the pound bought more at the end of Queen Victoria's reign than at the beginning. But the twentieth century has been different. Two major wars have been inflationary though prices fell in the inter-war period. The real escalator began in the late 1960s and moved so rapidly in the 1970s that the very fabric of society seemed threatened.

Nevertheless, by 1989 the scene was apparently transformed. Almost from nowhere Britain, and British business in particular, had leapt to the top of every league. The magazine, *Time*, ran a front page shouting 'Britain is Back'. The stock-market, even after a hiccup, rated Britain's businesses at five times the level of a decade earlier and in the cases of many relatively small companies at a hundred or even a thousand times their previous level. The shackles had been thrown off.

And the person receiving the credit was Margaret Thatcher. She had not succumbed to the defeatism of the seventies. She had identified the evils she perceived were afflicting the nation and had set out to destroy them. Her main targets were militant and mindless trade unionism and high taxation. One prevented management from managing, the other removed its incentive to do so. Through the early 1980s in a series of bloody set-piece confrontations culminating in the year-long battle with the National Union of Mineworkers and its demagogic leader, Arthur Scargill, she proved to managers that trade unions could be made to see sense. On the other hand the incentives to work hard and keep most of the rewards of that work were enhanced by the steady reduction in the rates of direct taxation, especially at the higher levels. In 1979 the standard rate of income tax was 33%, in 1989 it was 25%. In 1979 the highest rate of income tax was 70% with a supplement of 15% on 'unearned income', in 1989 it was 40% with no supplement.

There have been critics of this approach. It is apparently less caring and it does little to help those who cannot or will not stand on their own two feet. Nevertheless it undoubtedly unleashed in the majority a desire to work hard and be adequately rewarded for their work. For a minority it meant the opportunity for spectacular success and reward.

I was one of that minority. But was it therefore all due to Thatcherism that I was able to build a national company from a small local operation in and around Birmingham? For if Thatcherism unleashed all the pent-up forces, were not thousands of others waiting to build such companies in the funeral industry, my chosen profession? Why should I succeed so spectacularly where others have failed to grasp the opportunities? Would I have achieved it anyway, without the benefits of Thatcherism? And how was it that this self-confessed child of the 1960s – a decade with an obsession for discotheques, four-letter words, miniskirts, nudity, drugs, love festivals, cults and crazes – could become one of the most successful businessmen of the Thatcher decade and achieve great wealth?

Of course, wealth is not just about money. My greatest wealth is my wife and children. Success was always more important to me than money itself. I love winning and beating the opposition. The opposition isn't usually Ian Botham therefore I usually win. Financial wealth suggests different things to different people. To me it means never having to worry about the mortgage and perhaps being able to present programmes for the BBC – you need to be rich to afford their pay!

Whether it's success or financial wealth you desire, or both, read this book and go for it. The book will show you what can be done but only you can do it for yourself.

My book will give you a guide to achieve success *if* you have a positive attitude and pay attention to detail; if you don't, whatever your academic qualifications, it will not help you, because you can't help yourself. Without such qualities, you can only be a spectator, however knowledgeable a spectator, not a player, not a great achiever, and certainly not a star performer. Many people write business books – how many of them actually did it?

Well I did, not only once but I am now on the way to achieving it again with Hodgson Securities plc, a company I started with only £100,000; in so doing I incurred no bank gearing, paid myself back the £100,000 in the first year and will float in the next four years for £20 million, in a completely different industry to the one I achieved such success in on the first occasion.

Can your performance reflect this? Well perhaps. To do so requires an understanding of the importance of inner conviction, the motivation of others, the division of labour and responsibility and the essential attention to detail.

Qualifications are valuable but are only things that others award you; the inner conviction, the drive, the determination and enthusiasm must come from within you.

The university of Oxford gives you academic qualifications. The university of life gives you experience. The university of self-discipline and conviction that is free and in your head is the most important. Everything else you can learn as you develop but without such conviction you will *never* develop. Therefore the book is as much about inspiration as it is 'How to Become Dead Rich'

Motivation is absolutely essential when you enter the business arena, especially if you wish to build an empire, for the right reasons. You must have drive, determination and an amazing capacity for hard work. You must be capable of leading people and motivating them based on your words and the examples you set. You must have a positive attitude of mind with regard to your goals and at the same time be realistic in the knowledge that it is not just positive thinking but positive action and hard work that are going to get you there.

You must believe in yourself, your company and in your product. This is essential and any lack of belief in any of the above will present you with a fatal flaw in the very foundation of what you wish to create.

If on the other hand you wish to go into business primarily to be your own boss or because you don't like being told what to do, or because you would be able to choose hours to suit yourself, etc., etc., then you are most definitely going into business for the wrong reasons – with such selfish aspirations long-term success will be hard to achieve while short-term disaster may even be imminent.

Over the last years I have been honoured to become a patron of the Oxford Enterprise Society and indeed have addressed both that Society and its opposite number at Cambridge on more than one occasion. I mention this as it has always been a source of both amazement and amusement to me that the most common question I get asked is 'why should we bother to go to university – Richard Branson didn't, Alan Sugar didn't, you didn't, John Major didn't?' etc. My response to a student audience, much to the relief of the university tutors, is that education is a marvellous gift and that once having obtained their degrees, graduates can proceed with any business venture that they have in mind. The fact that most don't and instead become professionally employed indicates quite clearly that not everyone has the essential inner motivation.

In 1975 I bought from my father the ailing family funeral directing business for £14,000. On the first morning that I was able proudly to call myself Chief Executive I was sent for by the Midland Bank at Hockley, Birmingham, who promptly informed me in their opinion the company was insolvent. As a result they were going immediately to withdraw the overdraft facility and would be pleased if, as the new owner, I would put the company into liquidation so that the creditors could be satisfied by the sale of the Oaklands Funeral Home. Fortunately, I had prepared a plan and was able to explain it. Perhaps luckily for me the bank manager had got out of bed on the right side that morning and was willing to listen. At the end of the conversation he granted me an extension to the existing overdraft with the view to putting my plan into action. However, without inner motivation and conviction it is doubtful that I would have been able to convince him of the future that lay ahead for Hodgson & Sons Ltd.

I have always had drive, determination and motivation. I have always believed that the very best chance I had to win was to plan things out, stick to the plan and give it my best shot. The opposition – yes the opposition (anything or anybody in competition was always the opposition) – would not be working as hard as me and therefore I would win.

David Meakin, a business associate and a great friend for more than twenty years describes my philosophy simply, if somewhat unflatteringly –

> Howard does not always choose the easiest route. He may go via a rocky, bendy mountain pass while the other guy goes through the valley and down the motorway. Howard will drive on day and night knowing he is going to arrive. The other guy will stop at the motorway services for a break. The other guy will stop to look at the map and wonder if he is on the right road. Howard will get there first for sure. The other guy might not even arrive despite having chosen the better route. I have always been convinced that one of the most important reasons – in fact the foundations of Howard's success was his inner conviction – that inner motivation.

Love them or hate them the same quality can be seen in the make-up of most other successful entrepreneurs. Consider, for example, Richard Branson, Alan Sugar, Anita Roddick – all demonstrate the conviction in their beliefs, unstinting energy, and a determination to drive through their own policies even though, sometimes, the odds may be stacked against them.

The same clearly could be said of Margaret Thatcher. She wasn't right all of the time – who is? Businessmen like myself would certainly have urged her to take different routes on occasions. However, it cannot be denied that she acted always with conviction, determination and a highly developed sense of inner motivation. It was this energy and style which epitomised her tenure as a leader and motivator and she unquestionably inspired business-men like myself to depend upon one's own inner strength of motivation.

As the reader will have observed so far, I have emphasised the importance of 'inner motivation' as the key foundation upon which to build any successful enterprise. Now it might be useful to identify the source of my own self-confidence and assertive style – it hasn't all depended upon Margaret Thatcher. In piecing together the jigsaw of my career, the reader will be able to appreciate not only the ups but also the downs. I aim to show that with the right determination it might be possible – without qualification – for anybody to succeed in business – by trying!

HOWARD HODGSON

CHAPTER 1

BACKGROUND

Some people are born into businesses, some create businesses and others have businesses thrust upon them! My experience has been a heady mixture of all three. The question of survival in business and the progress towards success was in my case the result of a rapid learning curve. But let me start at the beginning.

Hodgson & Sons, the funeral directors, was founded in 1850 by my great-great-grandfather, who provided the financial backing, and his son, George, who expanded the business.

George, a charming, dapper little man, had moved to Birmingham from Sheffield to take up an apprenticeship with the large engineering business Guest, Keen & Nettlefold (now known as GKN). However, he soon saw greater potential in the family funeral business and abandoned his apprenticeship. After several liaisons, George married a woman who was a Romany queen, and the two moved into a flat above one of the firm's branch offices in Handsworth. Within a few years he was conducting no less than 3,000 funerals a year – thanks largely to the high birth and infant mortality rates of the nineteenth century.

George opened a series of branch offices, apparently installing a mistress in each one; it was suspected that the availability of a suitable mistress determined the location of a new office. After a time, George tired of the business, leaving it in the hands of his brother, who milked it before committing suicide. George returned with his two sons Osmond and Les, and soon after sold the business to his sons and Osmond's wife, Clarissa, who was a niece of the empire-builder Cecil Rhodes. To their consternation they discovered George had set up in competition with them ('no competition' clauses were not as common in sales contracts then as they are now). The young men were forced to undercut their father by quoting their clients three shillings (the equivalent of £10 in 1992) less than he did. Eventually the sons bought their father out again, and George retired to Brighton to concentrate on his two favourite pastimes; horses and women.

Osmond, Les, and Clarry incorporated the business into a limited company in 1923. At the beginning of the Second World War, Osmond and Clarry bought Les out. Les enjoyed a few years' success with an engineering company he set up mainly through government contracts during the War. By the time I was born in 1950 Les was in trouble, not for the first time, and was taken back into the firm, reluctantly by Osmond and only after persuasion from Paul, son of Osmond and my father, who was by then involved in the business.

From a nationwide perspective, Great Britain in 1950 was still wondering whether it was a world power. Following the Second World War, both Europe and Japan lay devastated; the United States was hovering between world involvement and a return to isolationism, and Britain – with most of its huge empire intact and sterling a reserve currency – was a leading player on the world stage, along with the USSR and America. The hard facts behind this façade, however, were different: Britain had lost £7,000 million, one-quarter of its entire wealth, during the War, and in 1947, after the first in a seemingly endless series of post-war sterling crises, the pound had been devalued against the dollar from $4.05 to $2.80.

Between autumn 1945 and summer 1947, six measures of public ownership were carried through Parliament: the Bank of England, cable and wireless, civil aviation, local electricity, and road and rail transportation. Gas, iron, and steel followed in 1950. This wholesale nationalization was the Labour government's answer to what they saw as the greedy exploitation by the bosses of the country's workers. Thirty years later, as Margaret Thatcher's government sold all but the Bank of England back to the people, not even the Labour Party raised much of a protest, confining itself to criticizing the government over the giveaway prices. Back in the 1940s, however, the cradle-to-the-grave interference and protection by the state had as few critics as it has defenders today.

I was fortunate to be born when the worst of the austerity was about to end. In the 1951 general election, a tired Labour Government was beaten and replaced by a Conservative administration more inclined to leave matters to the market. Rationing, which had been imposed on all staples, was gradually abandoned, and for most of my first ten years the country steadily became prosperous. Elizabeth II was crowned in June 1953, and at times – usually when the balance of payments was in surplus – there was talk of a second Elizabethan Age. Harold Macmillan was able to tell the voters, who returned yet another Tory administration to power in 1959, 'You've never had it so good.'

As the country prospered – even if it was beginning to slip behind its European rivals – the family business of Hodgson & Sons prospered with it. This was largely due to the unswerving professionalism of my father.

After a visit to the United States in 1963, he returned with his mind filled with what he had seen and learned about the funeral industry. What emerged was the Oaklands Funeral Home in Handsworth, with a range of facilities undreamed of in Britain. Funeral directors from all over travelled to admire the private-viewing chapels, service chapels, and selection rooms. He was also a striking symbol of unruffled dignity in the black tails and top hat that were his daily uniform as he led the funeral cortège.

In my small boy's way I used to watch the old man with the kind of reverence reserved for the Almighty. Yet perhaps I was quite right in doing so, because at that time a funeral director did almost have a God-like status in the tightknit community he served. No member of any other profession could hope to match the public's esteem of the local funeral director. He was part of the community in a way an accountant or solicitor never could be. He went into the homes of the bereaved, and helped them to cope with their grief; they in turn gave him the respect he deserved.

Osmond died in 1954, and my father took control of the business at the age of twenty-seven. Although initially he had been uncertain about his ability to take on such a business, he soon went from strength to strength, mainly because he was light-years ahead of his time.

Unfortunately, father started to lose interest in the business and handed over its day-to-day running to his right-hand man, meanwhile spending more and more time at clubs talking to other businessmen, who involved him in wildcat schemes.

While this was happening, changes were afoot in the country that also affected the business of Hodgson & Sons.

One factor that prevented Britain from competing effectively with its overseas rivals was the entrenched position of the trade unions, which had been given unique legal privileges in the Trade Disputes Act of 1906, and had used them regularly ever since. The incoming Conservative Government in 1951 spoke of dealing sternly with the unions and of repealing the 1906 Act. (The Heath Government in 1970 and the Thatcher Government of 1979 also campaigned with the same ideals.) In the end, however, the Tories backed off from confrontation. The Minister of Labour, Sir Walter Monckton, took on a role that meant maintaining close relations with the TUC, and setting up many courts of inquiry that usually gave the unions whatever they were asking for. As a result, the British disease of inflationary pay settlements with little advance in productivity became entrenched. By the 1960s, Britain's uncompetitiveness was beginning to cause ever more frequent sterling crises, as foreign holders of sterling worried alternatively about inflation, balance of payments deficits, and wildcat strikes.

The new Labour Administration of 1964, heralded in by Prime Minister Harold Wilson's promise of a 'white-hot technological revolution', adopted the same weak approach, with strikes being settled – always in the union's favour – informally over beer and sandwiches at Number Ten.

For every business inflation had become the norm, although during the 1950s and 1960s it averaged 4 and 5%, apart from two bad years early in the 1950s when the Korean War caused an explosion in the price of commodities and pushed the rate up to 9%. Nevertheless, the overall effect was corrosive. By 1970, the 1950 pound was worth less than ten shillings, or 50p as it would become with decimalization. Anything needing replacing would cost twice as much, in some cases more, and wage rates had risen much faster than the retail price index. For the moment, my father was not renewing much in the business but when he needed to he would have to generate a great deal more profit to be able to do so.

Demographic factors also were working against him. In Hockley, an area built during Joseph Chamberlain's expansion of Birmingham at the end of the nineteenth century, rows and rows of houses were being cleared to make way for new housing developments. The initial effect was a reduction in population, and even when the new houses were completed they would be occupied in the main by the younger generation. The end result was a reduction in the potential clientele for Hodgson & Sons. In Handsworth there was also a declining death rate due to a large influx of young immigrants. Kingstanding, where the firm also had a branch, was built in the 1930s, and also had a mainly young population.

One of the results of having a large overseas empire was that many inhabitants of the colonized countries wanted to come to the mother country. In the 1950s immigration into Britain began to climb, and in 1961 it had approached 150,000. The Conservative Government suddenly realized the implications of this, and introduced the Commonwealth Immigrant Act in 1962. The number of immigrants did not help Hodgson & Son because they were young and as a result had a low death rate.

While my father was coping with these problems, or leaving them to someone else, I was growing up. The eldest of three, I was in many ways a precocious child and typical of the generation of children born post-war. At the age of four I was sent to a small private school in a fashionable suburb of Birmingham. My school reports described me as a 'bone idle day-dreamer who lacks concentration'.

I remember home life as idyllic, though my parents were already beginning to squabble. At this time the firm was doing well, and the Hodgson household enjoyed the services of a cook, a nanny, a housekeeper, and a gardener. My father drove Jaguars – Marks 7 and 8 – and Armstrong Siddeley Sapphires. The old man also developed a passion for sailing, and joined the Poole Harbour Yacht Club in Dorset, where he entered with enthusiasm into both the sailing and social activities.

When I was eight I was sent to a preparatory school where the headmaster had taught my father. It was here at West House that I discovered I didn't like being told what to do; if there was authority, I simply had to challenge it. By the time I was twelve I was unchallenged as the worst-behaved boy in the school. Despite this I was made a prefect, and proceeded to exercise authority with the same enthusiasm with which I had previously flouted it.

Although I had never excelled, nor for that matter tried very hard, in the classroom, I had been reasonably successful on the games field and had won the cup for the best all-rounder, despite the fact that I suffered from asthma. By the time I was thirteen, medical experts insisted I be moved to a drier climate than Birmingham's. I was told that if I passed the common entrance exam I would go to father's old school, Malvern, a soccer-playing public school in the health-inspiring Malvern Hills. If not, I would go to the even healthier Swiss Alps. This concentrated my mind. The Swiss Alps held no appeal for me; they acted as a long-distance spur to my studies, which certainly needed something of the sort because I detested every subject except history. I derived tremendous satisfaction from reading about people like Charles II, Richard III, Napoleon and Bismarck. Their stories whetted my interest in power – although at that time, and for some years to come, whenever I met power in others it moved me to rebellion as if by automatic reflex.

I see myself as a child of my time, and indeed the 1960s was a decade of youthful rebellion. In place of the staid teenagers of the 1940s or the macho toughness of the fifties Teddy Boys the predominant theme of the 1960s was that of the more tolerant and feminine Mods who became notorious for their clashes with the more raucous Rockers at seaside resorts each Bank Holiday. Clothing, especially for girls, became more daring and provocative with skirts becoming shorter and shorter.

The new heroes and heroines were rebellious and, above all, young. There was no more powerful symbol than the Beatles, with Paul MacCartney, the most talented, fitting the ideal feminine attractiveness mould perfectly. Permissiveness was the rage and self-expression the god. Traditional disciplines, conveyed by parents, policemen, church leaders, school techers, employers or any other symbols of authority were to be disobeyed and derided.

Although I passed the common entrance exam at thirteen and was due to go to Malvern, because my asthma became very bad again in the winter of 1963–4 I was sent to Switzerland in May 1964. At fourteen years of age, I arrived at Aiglon College, Villars, 4,000 feet above Lake Geneva with a view facing Les Dents du Midi, a magnificent three-peaked mountain, and Mont Blanc.

Initially I was very homesick, but my skill at soccer proved a bonus, and an intelligence test revealed I had the second highest IQ in the school. Most of the other boys were American, the sons of film stars or business tycoons, and were at Aiglon either for their health or because it was not convenient for them to be at home. The school, run on the lines of Gordonstoun by a former Gordonstoun housemaster, imposed a rigorous regime. It had a ranking system rather like the army's, cold showers and press-ups in the snow were a prominent part of the routine, and we had to yawn our way out of bed at 6am in order to present ourselves for the 'treatment'. I shall never forget the day I managed to dodge the column because my hair was frozen to the window-sill at the head of my bed.

I continued in the style I had adopted at my previous school of putting most of my effort into games and rebelling against authority, although by the time I was fifteen the competitive urge was spreading from the games field to the classroom, and I enlisted the help of the school swot to get me into the A-stream, while I, in turn protected him from the bully-boys.

In the holidays I indulged in all the usual activities of a spoiled, middle-class teenager of the 1960s – chasing girls, smoking (in spite of my asthma, which was fast disappearing), drinking, and driving mummy's and daddy's cars, which I often bent. In 1966 I left Aiglon with this report:

> Howard is pompous, arrogant, self-opinionated, and inclined to think he is always right. He has small streaks of brilliance, but his ultimate success will be limited by narrow-minded drive and determination. Arrogance is no virtue, and he must learn this. He hates to be thwarted in his desires, but once he accepts it, he adjusts to the position manfully. There is a lot that is very good in him. He is courageous. I am sorry that he is leaving because I feel that he was just starting to find his feet here. If he turns out well it could be very good. However, if things go wrong with this boy, it will be very bad.

I left school with eight 'O' levels, and Birmingham Tutorial College was chosen to get me some 'A' levels. In the meantime, life in 1966 was still a huge joke – there were girls to be chased and football and cricket to be watched.

Immediately after England's victory in the 1966 World Cup Final I went to Majorca on a holiday with a friend. Returning from Majorca I started at the tutorial college, where my refusal to accept authority reached new heights – or depths. I was part of the outspoken generation that alarmed parents and teachers all over Britain. Free love, pot, 'flower power' and Carnaby Street made Twiggy's miniskirted London the swinging capital of the world. *Bonnie and Clyde* turned up on the cinema screens and became a cult. *Hair* arrived on the stage as a musical with full frontal nudity. My friends and I were rushing towards rebelliousness, tearing down accepted standards, mocking tradition, and saying 'no' to everything our parents were a part of. I am convinced that Britain's subsequent failure to compete economically with the Japanese and Germans stemmed from the laid-back, disinterested, uncompetitive kids of the 1960s, who turned their back on work and just did not want to know.

It is magnanimous of me to accept the blame for Britain's ills. In fact, the seeds of these ills had been sown long before the 1960s. Some believe, myself included, that they go back to the nineteenth century. There was no doubt, in any case, that by the end of the 'Swingin' '60s' they were becoming manifest.

Following the swingeing public expenditure cuts and taxation increases of July 1966, the British economy failed to improve, and by the autumn of 1967 yet another sterling crisis – partly brought on by the closure of the Suez Canal in the Six-Day War between Israel and Egypt – finally forced Wilson's Government to devalue the pound from $2.80 to $2.40. It was seen as a major national humiliation, made worse by Wilson talking about it on television as though it was some kind of victory for commonsense. It would be a victory, however, only if the necessary action was taken to restrain wage rises and improve managerial efficiency. Unfortunately, we were to wait many years and suffer many crises and humiliations before those conditions necesary for economic success were brought about.

In the meantime, I, along with most of the British population, was not ready for harsh reality. My behaviour at the tutorial college led the headmaster to telephone my father and sound a warning, although he added that provided I passed my 'A' levels, both Leeds and Nottingham Universities would accept me to read economics. In an attempt to instil some sense of responsibility, my father took me to see the family solicitor. Humiliated and defiant as ever, I told them I was not going to stay at college and take my 'A' levels, and I was not going to university:'I am going to leave here, get my hair cut, get a job and become a very successful man. Father, I am going to buy your business off you and save it from your foolish influence.' With that I slapped my top hat back on my head, buttoned up my military jacket, and left. My car ran out of petrol fifty yards from the office.

Despite my childish behaviour, my father accepted I did not want to go to university, and organized an apprenticeship for me with the Cardiff funeral director James Summers. I was first told I should have a haircut. Well-shorn, I began my apprenticeship in the coffin-fitting department, before progressing to the garage. From there I moved on to collecting the deceased for embalming in the firm's ambulance.

My first 'removal' was a frightful experience. We received the call just before lunch on a Saturday, when my thoughts were turning to the approaching weekend with my parents in Dorset. Instead, I found myself as a very raw rookie with two fully experienced companions making our way with a stretcher up to the top floor of a tower block. We introduced ourselves to the woman who opened the door. Without speaking, she motioned us to go into a room, but made no attempt to accompany us. As soon as we had entered, we realized why.

In one corner of the room was a corpse that clearly had been there far too long. The stench was indescribable. Not that we had long to think about it, because as soon as we went into the room, all three of us skidded and fell to our knees. The full horror of the situation became clear: the slippery mass on the floor was congealed blood, which had spread far and wide as a result of a massive haemorrhage; it was all over our clothes and squelching up through our fingers. While my companions were retching and heaving, I was unbelievably calm, only because in my ignorance I assumed that *every* removal was like this, and I had therefore better acclimatize myself very quickly, otherwise I would be letting my father down.

In fact, I came through with such flair that my two highly experienced companions had cause to wonder what kind of hard case I was.

It was some years after that that a Leeds councillor went on record with the thought that Leeds ought to have a municipal funeral service, because, compared with the city's municipal cemetery, that was the smart end of the funerals business. If he had slithered on that linoleum with me and my colleagues, I am sure he would have revised his ideas about keeping smart in the smart end.

Despite this baptism by fire, I stuck at my apprenticehip through the summer and autumn of 1968 progressing from coffin-fitter, to garage grease monkey, embalmer's assistant, office clerk, before being allowed to don a dark suit and actually go out on a funeral. By Christmas, however, I was becoming highly dissatisfied with my rôle as a pall-bearer. Progression seemed to have stopped. I wrote to the managing director and told him I thought the age of slave labour and benevolent despotism was over. This secured me the interview I had earlier been refused – and also earned me the sack. However, there was always the family firm. I began as assistant manager at Hodgson & Sons in January 1969.

At that time Hodgson & Sons was not as big as James Summers in Cardiff but the firm provided an unequalled standard of service. It was one of only seventeen in Britain to have become by invitation a member of National Selected Morticians, an organization based in the United States that demanded exceptional standards as a prerequisite of membership. By the time I joined, my father was no longer conducting funerals, leaving the public appearances in topper and tails to his managers.

I was soon to discover all the things that could go wrong on a funeral: the hired limousine that does not arrive; the hearse that breaks down; the grave that is too small for the coffin; the bereaved family that locks itself out of the house; the Asian family that sends the coffin out of the house without the lid on. While learning to cope with these little traumas, my father asked

me to take over the managership of Hartland & Son at Coseley in the Black
Country, a firm acquired in 1964. So, at the age of nineteen I became a
manager. I responded by applying Victorian management techniques,
which were, on hindsight, a little hypocritical, given my own previous
behaviour.

Due to the break-up of his marriage my relationship with my father
deteriorated. In 1970 he sacked me, whereupon I went to London and
joined the funeral director Ashton Ebbutt, a substantial firm conducting
2,000 funerals a year. Father soon regretted his action, and, realizing I was
making an essential contribution, invited me back to the family firm.
However, the reconciliation did not last long, and I moved into selling
holidays with Mato, a travel firm belonging to Doug Ellis, the chairman of
Aston Villa Football Club. Ellis put me in charge of the office in Cherry
Street, Birmingham, and paid me £20 a week (£200 a week in 1992).

Because I felt I could not survive on such wages, I answered an
advertisement that had been placed by an insurance broker called Tri-Star
Investments and promised earnings of £100 a week. It was soon apparent
that there *was* a life that suited me. In no time at all I had roped in my
friends and got them to form teams, starting by taking at least two new
people to an introductory meeting. They, too, enjoyed the challenge it
offered. But I was the one who was perched on the top of the heap, and who
rapidly established a reputation as the most go-ahead character in Tri-Star's
Birmingham branch.

By the end of 1971, I was so successful at Tri-Star that I left Mato
altogether and commuted to Stoke-on-Trent to run Tri-Star's office there.
Before long I moved to a competitor, North West Mercantile, and was soon
running the Birmingham branch and instituting my own style of leadership,
which reflected me rather than North West Mercantile.

The company certainly had never seen anything like the meetings I held
every Monday evening in Dr Johnson House in the centre of Birmingham.
The basic rule – my rule – was that once you had been to one meeting, you
had to return seven days later with two people whom you had persuaded to
join your team. Depending on how successful or otherwise your team had
been, you sat either near the front or near the back, so that nobody was in
any doubt about your competence, or lack of it, as a team leader.

Within three months, up to 500 people were turning up at these weekly
meetings. Facing the audience behind tables were the consultants, and
assistant branch managers, elevated according to rank on a series of raised
platforms. I was at the very top, the precocious twenty-two-year-old who
had planned it that way.

I operated on a mixture of charm and terror. For example, after
frightening an unfortunate underling to death by suddenly telling him to
stand up, I would announce that he had done particularly well in the

previous week, and encourage everybody to applaud his success. It was an outrageously stylized approach to management, but it worked. I was soon North West Mercantile's *enfant terrible* – and running the most successful branch in the country. My friends and I worked very hard. We were rewarded well. It was quite usual for me to earn £1,000 a week (£10,000 by 1992 standards).

The economy was growing well following the squeeze in 1968 and 1969, imposed by the Chancellor, Roy Jenkins. The Conservatives were re-elected in June 1970 and the new Prime Minister, Edward Heath, had talked tough at a Tory Conference in early 1970. However, in the face of collapsing business confidence and two possible major corporate catas-trophes at Rolls Royce and Upper Clyde Shipbuilders, Heath performed a U-turn, saved lame-duck companies with government money, and eased credit in the economy as a whole. The aim was to encourage investment in British manufacturing, but the result was speculation in financial instru-ments and in residential and commercial property. It was all to end in a spectacular bust at the end of 1973, but in the meantime money was available, people felt better off, and the climate was right for young and hard-working insurance salesmen. I grasped the opportunity, working eighteen hours a day, seven days a week. I genuinely believed that with a positive attitude, hard work, and team spirit I could lead normal, average people to success, and greatness.

My success in the Birmingham area led to my being given responsibility for North West Mercantile's new London office in 1972. While I was waiting for my new office, I stayed and operated from a hotel in Westbourne Terrace. It was there that I met my future wife, Marianne. The first meeting was not propitious.

I was in the room of two of my colleagues after a night on the town when one of them threw a pot of coffee against the wall. When there was a knock on the door, in vain I yelled 'Wait!' A Spanish chambermaid opened the door, which hit the coffee pot and sent it rolling across the carpet, spilling what was left of its contents before coming to rest against the soaked wall. 'I told you to wait. Now look what you have done,' I said. The chambermaid disappeared immediately, screaming at the top of her voice in Spanish. Soon afterwards, the French housekeeper stormed in, intent on avenging her abused subordinate. I tried to counter with an icy calm, as I pointed out she had no right to come into the room in that way. Not at all disconcerted, she said precisely what she thought about me and my attitude, spun on her heel, and started for the door. She made a highly charged exit, stage right.

That was my introduction to Marianne. It was memorable enough, but it paled in comparison with what happened at lunchtime that day in the hotel restaurant. I saw Marianne sitting a short distance away, so I decided to make her aware of my existence by throwing a lump of sugar at her. It hit her squarely on the back of the head, whereupon she jumped up, swung round, gave me a look of sheer contempt and fury, and yelled, 'Why don't you f . . . off?' I smiled shyly at the now silent restaurant; neither they nor I knew this woman was to become my wife.

Shortly after this I was fired for criticizing my bosses, in front of junior staff. However, it soon became clear that I was considered the prime motivating force behind most of their salesmen. I was invited back, but only on the basis that I become a director.

The hectic life continued. Marianne and I lived in a small, sparsely furnished flat in Birmingham. I travelled up and down the country all day, often arriving home at three in the morning and leaving again at eight. In August 1972 we were married at the parish church of Studley, Warwickshire. I conformed enough to have 'All things bright and beautiful' as the first hymn. After that my penchant for aggression and style took over with 'Onward Christian soldiers' and three Beatles songs to be sung during the signing of the register. Life continued, with me not easing up on my punishing schedule, but matters improved when we moved to a house in Manchester. On 20 December 1973 our first son – Howard James Paul – was born to be followed over the following seventeen years by two more sons, Charles and Jameson, and a daughter, Davina.

While I was working all hours, father was not working at all. His second marriage was worse than his first. Hodgson & Sons was running into serious trouble. By this time the number of funerals a year had dropped to 400. To counter this, my father bought a boat in Barbados but the charter business, which he had pictured his yacht the centre of, collapsed in no time when the man he had entrusted to look after it managed to blow up the engine. The problem was that in real life he was simply a highly professional funeral director whose head was in the clouds and who could not keep up with his own lifestyle.

Meanwhile, my father's secretary fought off creditors as best she could, while the cracks in the fabric of the firm began to widen. Time-scarred limousines were reliable only for the regularity with which they broke down; the chauffeurs and bearers – the walking advertisements for the firm – were wearing livery that had seen better days. In some desperation, my father asked me if I could lend him some money. Though I tried various finance houses, none were forthcoming. I then looked at the possibility of North West Mercantile buying the firm. They were looking to diversify, so why not the funeral business? A study of recent Hodgson accounts was why not.

It was then that a friend of mine said the magic words, 'You should be buying it for yourself, because you know how to run it.' He was right. I had grown up alongside the business; I had taken in my knowledge of funeral directing painlessly, through the pores, even though the financial anguish which the old man was putting both his business and himself through was to come as an almighty shock. And even when it came, it had not a hope of persuading me that my friend was not right: four generations of the Hodgson family had steered the firm already, and there was no need for anybody to persuade me that taking my turn would not be the most natural thing in the world.

At that time the prospect of taking the helm did not frighten or deter me. Years of hard work were on the cards, but hard work has never scared me. Nor have I ever been short of confidence – not even on the scale of confidence that was needed to save and then to build a business that my father, for all his professional expertise, had allowed to slide to the brink of bankruptcy. Back that confidence with pride in the family name and all it stood for and what you had was a twenty-five year old who saw that this business could and would be saved. I knew how to run the business, and I would do it: so, in 1975, I sold my house and bought father out for £14,000.

As my example suggests, to start your own business you do not have to have had wonderful school reports, academic qualifications and a perfect childhood. You *do* need conviction and a list of rules that must be obeyed.

CHAPTER 2

STARTING UP

Some people see an opening and decide to go into business. Others decide to go into business and need to find an opening. Either way, the type of business is important, and must be able to pass the following 'acid test'.

- Will you enjoy the business?

- Will you be good at it?

- Will it deliver good profits?

- Will there be a market in years to come?

- Will you be able to expand it?

The business you choose must score five out of five. If it does not, then look for another one. Less than five out of five means you are starting with a huge handicap which will condition your future plans.

STARTING UP, ACQUISITION, OR FRANCHISE?

Having decided the type of business, you should next think about whether you wish to start up a new business or acquire an existing one. Starting up vs. acquisition differs from business to business, and is something that must be carefully weighed up at the time.

Starting up has the advantage of a clean start, with everything organized in line with your thinking. Often it is cheaper as you have not had to acquire goodwill. On the other hand, the acquired business already has clients and profits and intangible assets. Although usually more expensive acquisition is often preferred by bankers, who will be asking you, 'Will the business work?', and 'Can you do it?' With the acquired business they at least know the business works by looking at its current trading.

You may be attracted to acquiring the business you currently work in but do not own. Management buy outs or MBOs as they are often referred to became very fashionable in the bull market and low gearing cost period of the '80s when all acquisitions seemed to be possible. Many were successful, as obviously, management knew the business and how to run it. Some failed because management sometimes did not understand finance. The gearing needed to affect the management buy out often starved the business of investment and working capital. Moreover more failed in the recession of the early nineties due to the fact that they were undertaken for the wrong reasons. They were not sensible, hard-headed investment decisions about a bright future but shareholders wanting out while management wanted to save its and everyone else's jobs by buying a failing business – theirs. I repeat you must go into business for the right reasons.

In 1990, 75% of new businesses failed, whereas only 6% of new franchises failed. That is a most impressive performance, but hardly surprising. Franchising has the best of both worlds: you get the support, help, and hand-holding that a national company can give, as well as the huge benefit of being part of a branded product. The franchisor is using someone else's money to expand, and knows that the people who run the branded branches really care because, unlike a large plc, they own their own business and are therefore dedicated to making it work.

Franchising therefore can be a safer and easier route. The franchise company often will help you to write your business plan, teach you how to present it, and may even help you source the funds to start up. They can be great hand-holders because they have lots of experience in location, legal matters, accounts, builders, bankers, loans, etc., all of which they are negotiating several times a year. Moreover they will give you and your required staff product and marketing training and usually a fair amount of advice as you get going out in the field. They want you to succeed because your success adds to theirs.

Another reason why franchises tend to succeed is that the franchise companies usually insist that you put enough capital into the business in the first place. This, and the high-street image of most successful franchises, ensures that the business gets through the difficult early period. Lack of start-up cash, and using this unwisely, are the major reasons for new-business failure. All too good to be true? Well, remember that with all of that back-up and high chances of success you cannot buy a franchise in a successful company for peanuts.

If you feel this suits you, then a visit to one of the national franchise exhibitions is a must. The British Franchise Association offers helpful advice on every aspect of franchising, and should be contacted for further information.

Not everyone is a great fan of franchising. Indeed, Sophie Mirman, co-creator with her husband Richard Ross of Sock Shop has queried its value from a franchisor point of view in Debbie Moore's book *When a Woman Means Business*. She worried about quality control. However Sock Shop only had two franchise shops and should have tried harder to overcome their problems in that area as the development of a successful franchise expansion along the lines of Body Shop International would have ensured that Richard and Sophie still had control today of their creation.

How does franchising exactly work? Why is it so successful? And why am I so keen on it? Well, in 1991 I launched a new group of companies under the banner of Hodgson Securities plc. One of these is called Prontac. Prontac presents an exciting new franchise opportunity for the business entrant.

Prontac is a new, inexpensive service which has been designed to provide speedy and accurate accounts and VAT returns for small businesses.

Prontac combines high technology with a personal service in the convenience of their own place of work thereby saving small businesses from the headache of accounts production.

Historically, small businesses have either had to hire expensive book-keepers or spend valuable time on routine paperwork. Either way there has been a considerable delay in the production of essential accounts.

Prontac addresses this need efficiently and at a low cost. Computerised accounts are normally delivered within seven days of data collection and accurate and speedy VAT returns will be delivered in a format acceptable to the VAT authorities.

Prontac franchises its operation to successful applicants with no geographical limitation. The initial franchise includes the supply of computer hardware, licence to use Prontac software, full training for the franchisee and his staff, national computer bureau back-up, the formation of his own limited company and access to a marketing support team.

Applicants have no need for previous experience in computing or accountancy as this work is undertaken by the dedicated computer bureau. Prontac therefore provides an excellent business opportunity to a wide variety of people for an investment of just £12,750.

Knowing what I know now I would strongly recommend the franchising route as a positive entry into business. Franchisor and franchisee, each owning their own business, yet with common goals, working in harmony to win and no bloody middle management in sight. Wonderful.

SOLICITORS

You must take independent legal advice when starting your business. In particular, you will need advice about setting up the limited company, partnership, or sole tradership, and all matters regarding your location, such as conveyance, change of use (if applicable), and planning permission. Cutting corners could prove to be very expensive later on. Imagine, two years down the road and your business is well established on your site and, bang, you discover you have always needed a planning permission that you do not have.

It is important to choose your solicitor carefully. He or she need not be expensive or work for a large, well-known name, but they must be dealing with small corporate work all of the time to ensure having the job well done and getting value for money. The country is littered with solicitors who may be jolly good at other things, but do not know enough to advise you on these matters – and you certainly do not want the blind leading the blind at this stage.

Either way you must feel comfortable with your solicitor. You should like him, trust him and enjoy working with him. As your business expands you may well have to see a lot of him. He will become part of your team. Therefore make enquiries, check things out and look around before making a decision. Whatever you do don't do what I did. My first solicitor was my father's (oh, I really searched hard for him, didn't I?) and he treated me like a little boy and my second was a friend who went to prison for dipping into the client account. My first choice didn't really help me, while my second did me much harm as both my company's money and mine were in the 'looted' client account. It took a lot of distracting hard work to get it all back – which I did with interest – but it was all so stressful and hurtful and my fault for not selecting a solicitor carefully enough in the first place.

If your business is to be a limited company, then the question of a company secretary should be discussed. Running your limited company legally and correctly is important. Your solicitor or accountant may be suitable for the company secretary post. If so, then do a deal on fees. In other words, lower fees now because of the annual fee for being company secretary. Never be frightened to barter with solicitors or accountants.

LOCATION

Location is either very important or irrelevant. It is really about what your business does and where the competition is, as well as the availability of labour. If location is important, then you must weigh the pros and cons between a prime site and high rent against a good site with a lower rent.

Other points should be taken into account as well, such as parking, security, and what the other shops near you do. If you plan to sell religious books, do you want to be surrounded by massage parlours? A Chinese takeaway does not want to be next door to a funeral director, and a funeral director certainly does not want to be next to a Chinese takeaway!

Wherever you go and whatever you do – get the correct planning permission before you start.

FITTING OUT

Always get three quotes for everything. Apply this rule today and for ever more about everything you need to buy. Having decided who wins, and remember it is not necessarily the company that gave the cheapest price, make a nuisance of yourself when it comes to seeing the fitting out through. Ensure that the quality and quantity of work undertaken matches what was written in the quote, and do not make the final payment until the builder has completed everything on your 'snag list'. I have never known a builder yet who can finish a refurbishment without failing to see hundreds of small mistakes.

FREEHOLD OR LEASHOLD?

Freehold is fine if you can afford it. Your business will have a stronger asset base, and you will not have rent to pay. Moreover, that asset may be used as security when borrowing for expansion. However property values can go down as well as up as we have learned in the nineties and that may prove to be a bad investment and could even cause the bank to withdraw its support; furthermore you will probably be starting your business with limited funds, and will need all the cash you can muster to work for you from day one, and therefore will need to look at leasehold.

Licence? Short-term or long-term lease? Value? Premium? Rent-free period? Insurance? Responsibility of repair and decoration? Rent increases? Clauses concerning mode of operation? All of these points and many more must be considered. *Get proper legal advice before signing anything.* Either way barter. Especially now (1992) while there is over-capacity in the market place. There are some very good deals to be had. Recently I negotiated for a suite of offices in St Helens Place, Bishopsgate, opposite the Stock Exchange. Rents there had been as high as £65 per square foot. But not today. Now the landlords only wanted £35 a square foot on a sixteen-year lease. When I had completed negotiation they settled for £20 per square foot, with a 8-year break clause in our favour, 2 years rent free, the service charge capped for 4 years and all the partitioning to be paid for by them. Good saving yes? Never, never just accept what is offered by the other side.

ACCOUNTANTS

Like solicitors, accountants do not have to come from the 'big six' (e.g. Price Waterhouse, Arthur Andersen, etc.). However, you must feel confident they can give you sound corporate advice, help you with your business plan, and be very much on the ball regarding tax and tax relief. As with the solicitor, talk money early on and do not accept 'we will tell you how much the bill will be when we know'. The chances are that you will not be behaving like that with your clients, so do not let them act like that with you!

The 'big six' have huge resources, experience and ability but for a new business they may be a bit expensive and impersonal. Moreover you, as a new small business are hardly likely to get the most senior man on your account. On the other hand do not go to a 'back street' small practitioner. His bills may be the cheapest but the cost to you via 'cock ups' could make him very expensive. I would recommend a well-established firm in your town that has nevertheless got some young faces in it. Listen to accountants' advice when you are not sure if you are right. Never listen when you know you are right. This rule has stood me in good stead for two decades.

THE NAME AND LOGO

Your business's name should represent you, or what you do, or both. It should be memorable and simple. It should not be irrelevant, make extravagant claims, or be based on a fashion that could disappear in a matter of months or years. Avoid corporate logos – the name should be the logo. IBM is the classic example: it is simple, memorable, and the computer-paper effect tells you exactly what they do. The identity is the name; the name is the identity – simple and inseparable. When you are famous you may spend a lot of money getting a design agency to plan your logo; for the moment, think it out yourself, and save your money.

Once you have agreed upon a name, turn your attention to corporate colours, typeface, and how your business is going to express itself. Remember that anything to be printed in more than one colour will be more expensive. The typography chosen should always be consistent on letterheads, brochures, shop signs, and so on. You need to paint things so use the corporate colours; you need signs in corporate colours and typeface; you need letterheads, business cards, and sales literature using the corporate colours, typeface, and consistent use of language. Choose colours with these points in mind, and be careful not to choose fashionable colours that could date quickly.

DRESS

Now that you are going into business seriously, look seriously businesslike. Dress smartly and appear crisp and clean. You do not have to be too conventional – I mean how dare I (of all people given press comment about my suits, hair, etc.) say that to you – unless the business demands it. The press forgets that the 'flamboyant Hodgson' spent over a decade as an extremely smart, short-haired, top-hatted, tail-coated funeral director. The business demanded it and I gave it because I realized that was the professional thing to do. The clients expected it and thus would perhaps have not realized how keen I was to look after their interest if I had given the wrong impression by my dress. In terms of building an image, however, dress can matter. Look at Richard Branson with his laid-back look, all cardigans and Levis, or John Harvey Jones with his long hair and flamboyant ties.

STAFF

You may be able to start up in business on your own without staff. On the other hand, if from day one you need assistance, and how much will be clear from your business plan, then staff should be chosen carefully, and not taken on until your business plan has been accepted and you are ready to open up.

If your business is a specialist one, then using a specialist employment agency may be the answer. However, watch the expense; you can always save the fee by placing an advertisement in a relevant publication.

Interview as many people as necessary until you find staff you are happy with. If that does not happen with the first advert, then do not employ 'the best of the bad bunch'. Repeat the exercise until you find the person, or people, you feel comfortable with.

Naturally, staff must be decent, honest, hardworking, loyal, and give the impression you wish the clientele to receive. This is easier said than done. Trust your judgement: you must feel at ease with an employee; you must like him or her; you must trust him or her; you must know that you will be able to tell them what to do and you must know that they will obey.

Trust your judgement, but give yourself the best chance by always taking up references and carefully reading cvs. You do not have to be too influenced by a cv, but read it and ask the relevant questions. It contains a life, and should tell you a lot about the person.

Having made the choice always start staff on a probation period. Ensure you issue them with a proper employment contract and that you are familiar with industrial law and their rights under it concerning such things as maternity leave, sickness, retirement, etc. Look after your staff and they may look after you. Don't and they certainly won't.

If you are acquiring a business then you are almost certainly getting the staff with the business. Look at them both individually and in total very carefully before deciding to proceed. Under British law you are stuck with them, and to get unstuck you may have to pay a lot of redundancy on top of the purchase price.

RETAIL PRICING AND TRENDS

If you will be setting the retail price of your product, look carefully at the prices charged by your competitors. Aim to increase your gross margins by controlling costs, and if possible offering a wider range, rather than overpricing the products. On the other hand, be careful not to cut the price too much. High turnover with no profits, or even losses, is a trap that many fall into. Once the price is set, it must go forward into your business plan. If you decide to alter the price, you must alter the cash-flow forecasts and profit-and-loss projections in your business plan. Failure to do so renders your plan useless.

Watch your market and your competitors. Join trade associations, and perhaps the local chamber of commerce. You will not agree with all that you see or hear, but at least you will know what is going on. You must make every effort to get ahead and stay ahead. Do not confuse this with continually worrying about 'what the opposition is up to'; you worry about your business, and let them worry about theirs.

Always remember the opposition, when you talk to it, is full of bullshit. Everybody always says how well they are doing. When I first owned Hodgson & Sons Ltd I used to bump into other funeral directors – usually at West Brom or Perry Barr Crem. They were always so busy. They all seemed to be doing so much better than me. However I soon realized that if they had all been telling the truth then half the population of Birmingham would have 'kicked the bucket' that week. If you really want to know what they are doing then send off to Companies House for a set of their accounts.

MARKETING

All business whether it is 'service' or 'production' is really only about 'manufacturing' and 'distribution'. For example, even if your business is public relations, the service you give is your 'manufacturing' and how you sell it is your 'distribution'. 'Manufacturing' is useless, loss-making and pointless without 'distribution'. You have to sell your product or service. Know who is your client and how you are going to reach him. Target your market: this may be best achieved through advertising (which is dealt with later) or by engaging a sales force. If the latter then firstly ensure the force is properly trained. They must believe in the product and the company. They must know about the product and how to market it. Then you must organise them in order that you get optimum performance out of their labours. Running a marketing force is half about motivation and half about attention to detail.

The salesmen must phone in each night to discuss the day's appointments. You must have devised forms on which such data can be recorded in order to capture information on which you can formulate your opinions concerning marketing ratios, etc., and your sales team's performance by comparison to them. Pay attention to detail. Go through the results of the day's appointments with your staff. If needed, smash them into the ground, go through it with them, before picking them up and motivating them so they can't wait to go to bed, to get up the next day and do it all perfectly.

As your sales force grows introduce targets, incentives, competition and meetings. Targets for individuals and teams to strive for. Competition because they will strive harder if frightened someone else will be there first and a weekly meeting becomes a stage where all of this can be acted out.

At such meetings announce the league table position of the various levels of marketing personnel you have – i.e. a league table of Salesmen, a league table of Sales Managers and a league table of Regional Sales Managers, etc. This way you get healthy competition throughout each level of the marketing force. People will work hard for individual or team goals when victory ensures applause and praise at next week's meeting. Positions should be announced each week but the 'season' should last a month before restarting. A week is too short, a year too long.

We have already heard how successful Prontac became when I launched Hodgson Securities plc, but this success was rivalled by its sister subsidiary company Hodgson Integrity Ltd, a financial services company. The company is divided into two divisions. A sales operation marketing specially designed financial service products to a conventional 'client base', i.e. aged between 20 and 50, and secondly, a mature or third age marketing force, recruited specifically to market a tailored product range to over fifties clients. This second division will not commence activities until the spring of 1992. However the conventional 20 to 50 marketing force started to be recruited in September 1991 armed with a specifically designed product range under the banner of 'Hodgson Integrity' and underwritten by Eurolife. The staff (called advisors) were carefully trained under the rules of LAUTRO for the purposes of compliance and then again for each product. At each stage they had to pass an exam. Each new advisor was then accompanied in the field when making appointments and writing business until they became proficient. Once they have written 10 plans they may apply to be a manager. They will then receive management training and have new recruits placed in their team. They will be responsible for these people just as their manager had been responsible for them. They will receive override commission on business written by people in their team.

When they have six people in their team and provided that the team is writing more than 40 plans a month collectively then they qualify for Unit Manager status and can receive override on staff in their team members' teams. If their direct team falls below 6 or they fail to write 40 plans collectively in a month they will lose Unit Management status. Once the required performance has been sustained for 6 months they qualify, provided their lapse rate is below 10%, for Regional Manager Designate status which in itself gives them access to a company car.

These then are their targets. The offices update the league tables for new trainees, Advisors, Managers and Regional Sales Managers daily. Competition is fierce at the weekly meetings and once a month the winners get a certificate and hold the cup on their desk for the next month. Sometimes I think the winners care more about the cup than the money they have earned. However due to the lapse rate qualification quality of business is maintained. Moreover the staff while competing internally, unite externally to be proud of this brave new company and enjoy great rivalry with Prontac.

It is clear that you must carefully research what you want to do and where you want to do it. Is this kind of business really successful? How successful is the competition? Why are they successful? Where are they situated? How many of them are there in your town? Are some more successful than others? If so, why? Is there going to be enough 'easy' parking? Can you generate the turnover quickly enough to pay the rent? You must ask and answer all of these questions and many more. Once you have the answers, you need to write a detailed business plan.

THE PLAN

Okay, so we now believe in ourselves, our company, and our product. We have drive, we have determination, we have a positive attitude. We have understood the essential component parts of putting the business together. We are going to work hard and create team spirit. What now? We must have a plan that we operate by, and a plan we are able to show to banks in order to raise the necessary capital.

You will need to think about the following:

● **A five-year strategy with aims and objectives.**
Where do you want to be in five years' time? Would you like to eventually float the company on the Stock Market? How big do you want to build it? Are you going to keep it or ultimately will you wish to sell it? Ask yourself these questions, answer them, and you will have the basis of your strategy.

- **A business plan**. A detailed business plan has to be written expertly and concisely, with the logic and accuracy of each statement carefully vetted. It must provide clearly defined aims, and a coherent route to achieving them.

- **A two-page explanation about who you are and what your company does**. Write this carefully and take care with presentation. Often this is the first important impression you give to clients, bankers, and so on.

- **Financial information**. You need a profit-and-loss account, a proforma balance sheet, and a cash-flow forecast. You need these to take to a bank in order to borrow capital for your venture. But that is not their only purpose: these are your management tools, and they should be used by you continually in the running of your business. Moreover, they should be constantly updated to reflect the current position of your business. You must have monthly management accounts – however small your business is.

- **Capitalization**. Often, it is due to under-capitalization that new businesses do not progress, or even fail. It is important to ensure that a new business is not starved of capital, therefore it is important to obtain the correct level of investment right from the beginning. If this cannot be achieved on your own or with bank gearing, then seriously consider taking on a partner. It is better to own half of a successful venture than all of a failed venture.

- **Optimum level**. Ensure from day one that your business is lean and fit and running at an optimum level. Having put into place the correct investment level, do not waste the same on unnecessary expenditure. Impress upon staff it is cheaper to phone in the afternoon, etc. Your control of fixed overhead costs, such as gas, electricity, telephones, staff, etc. is essential.

- **Stock**. Get your levels right. This means as low as possible without risking production or delivery to the client. Remember, excessive stock is your cash tied up.

- **Marketing**. Target your market. Research in advance where your best marketing returns are likely to come from. Advertising can be extremely expensive, especially for a new, small company. You cannot afford to waste money on advertising that does not give you the highest possible marketing ratio. If you need to buy space regularly then get a media buying agency to do this for you as they will be able to get you high discounts to the quoted 'card' rate. Moreover if you don't need to be in a certain newspaper on a certain day then allow the agency to shop around and leave it late as massive discounts are available just before the paper 'goes to press'. Run a variety of adverts and monitor results. Settle on your most successful but always try new ones every now and then to see if they can beat your current successful ad. Adverts are expensive so ensure the 'leads' which result are treated like gold.

- **Sales invoices**. Invoice promptly and collect debts quickly. Do not give extended credit. Do not take on and continue to deal with poor payers. This is along with under-capitalization and lack of management accounts perhaps the greatest reason for new-company failure. I used to look at our outstanding accounts daily, putting aside at least half an hour just for this purpose. The more you ignore the problem, the bigger it will become. Stick to your terms of trade and give a discount for early settlement.

- **Purchase invoices**. Negotiate the best price, delivery, and credit terms for the quality you require. Stick to the terms, but do not pay more, or more frequently, than you have to. It is better to drive a hard bargain and keep to it than to attempt to get more credit by ignoring the statements and lose your supplier. As with your bankers, always communicate with your suppliers. They are much more likely to be helpful at a time of crisis if they know and trust you.

- **Income stream**. Where possible, put into place an income stream for your business before it starts up. If you start your business without any idea where the first order is going to come from, valuable capital can be wasted simply meeting day-to-day running costs before sales are achieved.

- **Government help**. You will certainly be able to get advice, and perhaps even financial help, from your local government enterprise agency. The DTI enterprise initiative, supported by your local chamber of commerce and many other organizations, is there to help you. They want you to succeed, so go and see them. This could be time very well spent.

Armed with your five-year strategy, your two-page report, your profit-and-loss account, balance sheet, and cash-flow, you have a business plan. And because you believe in your plan, you can sell it to investors/bankers, who will be impressed not only by your drive, determination, and enthusiasm, but by the professional way you have thought things through. Always be prepared to demonstrate your belief in your plan. You must be able to answer all questions concerning it, so ask yourself and answer every possible question before making a presentation. Even better, get your accountant or financial adviser to test you before you go to a bank.

Be objective. Do not sweep a flaw in the plan under the carpet. A flaw could cause your bankers and investors to lose, but also the largest investor of time, money, energy, and reputation is *you*. Always be honest, especially with yourself.

THE PRESENTATION

Before making a presentation draw up a list of bankers and/or investors that you wish to see. Put the most important people high in the order but not at the top of the list as you do not want to make your first presentation to them. You will be so much better at it by the time you have done four or five of them. Never, never see more than one party at a time. Imagine if you had three interested investors and you saw them all together and then made a bad presentation. You may have killed the whole idea. On the other hand a bad presentation to the first can be put right before you see the next two. Always plan in advance your timescale so that you are not in a desperate hurry for the investment. 'Desperate hurriers' put investors off.

When making a presentation you need to make three points: what you do, how you do it, and the 'back-up financials'. The meeting may last one or two hours, but that should be because of the interest taken in your plan and thus the questions asked – the actual presentation should not be longer than ten minutes. It should include as much visual aid as possible. Videos, stills, slides, pictures, drawings, etc., should be professionally produced, and introduced during the presentation in a way that they are an *aid* to and not a distraction from, the message you wish to get across.

A good presentation does not make up for a bad plan, nor does it guarantee that a bank will agree to grant you what you require. On the other hand, a bad presentation could disguise a good plan and prevent a bank from lending to you. Give yourself the best possible chance by having a clear plan and presenting it professionally.

In your future dealings with the bank, always keep the manager informed. Admit to problems when you become aware of them. He is there to help you and he will certainly respect you more than if you either conceal problems or fail to answer his calls. I always treated the bank as part of the team.

CHAPTER 3

MOVING FORWARD

The world had changed a great deal when I bought Hodgson & Sons from my father. In the previous eighteen months Britain had expanded into what became known as the 'Barber Boom'. Anthony Barber, now Lord Barber, was then Chancellor of the Exchequer in Edward Heath's Government, and in 1971 and 1972 had pumped money into the economy. Unfortunately, the whole world was booming together, largely on the back of an inflationary boom in the United States. This was caused by the Johnson and Nixon Administrations paying for the increasingly expensive involvement of the United States in Vietnam, not by raising taxes but by printing money.

In 1971 the United States turned from being an exporter of oil into an importer. In October 1973, when the Yom Kippur War broke out, the Arab oil producers chose to quadruple the price of oil and to cut back production. The effect on world trade was disastrous. Both industry and consumers had become extremely profligate in their use of oil, which had been getting cheaper and cheaper over the previous decade. Now it was suddenly expensive and, some believed, in short supply. Some panicked, others speculated, and the price of oil rocketed. It was as though the whole world had received a massive increase in its taxes. Tens of billions of pounds, dollars, deutschmarks, francs, and lira were taken out of the world economy and put into the Arabian desert. Until this money could be recycled into the system, the world was going to suffer.

And suffer it did. Britain, because of its continuing structural weaknesses, suffered more than most. The 'Barber Boom' had not worked. British manufacturers had not invested as much as had been hoped, and the two main results of the expansion in credit had been an explosion in property prices and a rapid increase in inflation. This fuelled resentment from the wage- and salary-earning classes, who did not benefit from rising property and stock-market prices, and who felt the impact of rising prices in the shops.

In an attempt to choke off inflation, Heath's Government tackled the symptoms – rising prices, dividends, and earnings – without tackling the cause – too much money. In the autumn of 1973, just before the oil crisis, the government introduced stage one of an incomes policy that would allow index-linked rises if inflation rose about 7%. Thanks to the oil-price hike, inflation rose quickly above that level, and automatic pay rises produced a ratchet effect, pushing it higher and higher. The National Union of Mineworkers (NUM) had learnt the lesson of craven collapses when faced with union pressure by both governments since the War and especially of the present government when faced with their own demands in the early part of 1972.

The National Union of Mineworkers (NUM) submitted a large pay claim and imposed an overtime ban on 8 November 1973. Heath panicked, and declared a state of emergency on 13 November. A month later he declared a three-day week to preserve fuel, and though negotiations with both the Arabs and the miners continued, the only results were the continuation of high oil prices and a miners' strike. In the end and, for some, three weeks too late, Heath called an election with the implied platform of 'Who governs the country, the government or the unions?'

The electorate was not sure who should govern the country – the Tories, who at long last had shown some signs of standing up to the unions, or the Labour Party, who might at least get them back to work – and gave neither party an overall majority, but more seats to Labour than to the Tories. Heath tried to negotiate with the Liberal leader Jeremy Thorpe to form a coalition, but Thorpe would not play, and Labour, under Harold Wilson, formed his third administration.

When the Labour Government gave in to the NUM, the rest of the unions followed in a rush, sending inflation soaring to 25%. While inflation soared and everyone tried to keep pace, financial institutions, and to a lesser extent manufacturing businesses, were suffering severely from the financial squeeze that had been imposed in the autumn of 1973. Nearly all of the secondary banks went into liquidation or were rescued by the main banks, prompted by the Bank of England. Even the National Westminster Bank was forced to make a formal denial that it was in trouble. If the new Chancellor, Denis Healey, had not introduced a corporate tax-saving measure – stock relief – many manufacturing companies would have failed. On the London Stock Exchange, prices fell throughout 1974, and the *Financial Times* thirty-share index fell to 147 in early January 1975 (it had been over 500 as long ago as 1968).

As well as giving way to every pay demand between March 1974 and the summer of 1975, the Labour Government gave the unions enormous privileges, which were to prove extremely costly later in the decade and in the early 1980s. The Trade Union and Labour Relations Act of 1975, masterminded by the left-wing Michael Foot (later to be elected leader of the Labour Party, much to the delight of the Tories), granted the unions privileges not enjoyed by any institution in Britain since the Church before the Reformation. For example this law meant that unions would no longer be liable for damage inflicted as the result of an industrial 'dispute' even where the victim had nothing to do with the dispute.

These were the prevailing political and economic circumstances when I bought Hodgson's and went to see the firm's bank. It disproves the theory that you can only make a successful presentation when the economy is in a comfortable state. Therefore, if you are thinking, 'Well, he never had the 1990 recession to worry about', you are wrong, it was far worse.

My father had been streets ahead in the way he had handled his responsibilities to the bereaved. But I was the first to see that with funeral businesses, as with marriages, two could live as cheaply as one: if there are, say, half-a-dozen small businesses in an area, there are enormous possibilities if they are grouped as partners rather than rivals, with a massive reduction in the capital outlay that is involved in keeping them separate.

Every funeral business needs a hearse, a couple of limousines, a removal vehicle, garages, a receptionist, liveried staff, a mortuary, a chapel of rest, and all the other accoutrements of the profession. I realized there was no reason why many of these should not be shared by several funeral homes, with the benefit of tremendous economies. As separate entities they each were faced with the burden of meeting outgoings, of which 80% were the same every week, whether they handled one funeral or half-a-dozen. To improve their revenue, they would have to handle more funerals, but with too many businesses already in the field, and no prospect of a surge in the death rate, this was not possible.

My vision was to unite small clusters of independent businesses into the Hodgson empire. (That was a terribly grand-sounding word for what was in 1975 a little family concern whose public image had been allowed to become distinctly frayed because there was no money available for new limousines, new uniforms or anything else – but that was my vision.) My problem was that I not only had to impress upon a bank manager that it was a practical plan and that I was capable of achieving it, I also had to dissuade him from closing the company down.

The hard facts I faced when I met him were that Hodgson & Sons had an agreed overdraft facility of £9,000 but was £14,000 overdrawn. Not only had nothing been done in response to repeated requests to reduce the overdraft, but my father had completely blotted his copybook by not going anywhere near the bank to discuss the situation – bank managers do *not* like to feel ignored at such times.

When the manager told me he did not have a lot of sympathy for Hodgson & Sons, and was in fact going to close the company down, I could see his point. The firm had creditors of more than £100,000, and £14,000 which it claimed as being owed were not debtors but money owed by a subsidiary company. Worse, the boat business in Barbados owed money on both sides of the Atlantic, and was also a wholly owned subsidiary. Listed among the assets was a van that was on hire purchase, and a car that was driven away and never seen again. My father had a second mortgage on his home at 8% above base rate. Vast amounts of money had been going out of the firm, and its creditors were increasing because income was not even covering the interest owed to various banks. Ironically it seemed as if I would be soon attending the company's funeral.

All I could offer was my self-confidence, my pride in the family name, my ideas on rationalization and my business plan. Why should I watch small, independent businesses struggling in competition with each other, all of them having highly valuable vehicles, refrigerated units, embalming facilities and staff, when I was sure that by amalgamating some of those assets I could run perhaps five of them as cheaply as one? At current prices, the half-dozen funerals a week that a small business might expect to handle would bring in about £3,000, and involve about forty manhours each, but five firms could bring in £15,000 for the same amount of equipment and hardly any increase in staff. This would make possible improvements in standards of service, which could not otherwise have been achieved, and enable those improved standards to be offered more cheaply.

An important part of my strategy was to keep the original names of any businesses I acquired, along with the people who sat in the front offices. Families have a tremendous loyalty to funeral businesses: once a firm has brought its expertise to a family in its grief, if there are subsequent bereavements in that family, it will consult the same firm almost as a matter of course. This was certainly true then, if somewhat less so today because of population mobility. There would have been no future in taking the name Hodgson into an area where it was not known and where it had attracted no loyalty. The name over the door was all-important, and would be retained. Nothing would have changed except the quality of service would be improved.

I told the bank manager there would be no difficulty persuading firms to sell out to me. Twenty years earlier, funeral directors were doing nicely, with a funeral costing nine times the average weekly wage. But because inflation had overtaken them – largely due to their own lack of business acumen – the cost of a funeral was now less than three times the weekly wage. There were also far too many firms in competition. I knew there were funeral directors who would be only too happy to call it a day.

I had made a good presentation. The manager granted me a stay of execution, and increased the overdraft facility to £20,000 and Hodgson & Sons Ltd (established 1850) had a chance to survive.

The first thing I did was to call all the staff together, and after firing one young man in the habit of going home early, told them that if any of them were planning on behaving similarly, they would be better off joining him, because all I could offer was blood, sweat, and tears.

One of my first actions was to invite John Taylor, who I had met at Tri-Star and who had gone to work for me at North West Mercantile, to come and work for me as a personal assistant. Taylor remembers that the first months were very difficult:

> The lead had been stolen from the roof and it leaked. The base of the body of the removal van was held together by welded cocoa tins. Howard conducted the funerals and I was his PA. We both washed the cars, which consisted of two hearses, a Rolls Royce, and a Humber, and two Ford limousines. We had to rely on a lot of part-time staff. We would do as many as seven funerals a day, and in between pick up bodies and then at the end of it wash the cars.

John McManus, who became a regional director of PHKI (PFG Hodgson Kenyon International plc), joined Hodgson & Sons in 1977 and recalled that the white van had been bought secondhand from a builder and that the Rolls Royce hearse was 25 years old. He started as a part-time driver and was paid £1 a funeral. (A part-time driver in 1991 could earn £15 a funeral.)

Perhaps this was not a great beginning, what with leaky roofs, old hearses, limousines that often broke down, a secondhand builder's van for an ambulance, sulky staff, and no money to put any of it right, but we had a plan and we presented it well. Moreover I got the concept across clearly in the first ten minutes of the meeting with the bank manager and despite the appalling condition of the economy and the failed state of Hodgson & Sons we got what we wanted – bank support. Moreover, we had more or less adopted the twelve points mentioned in the previous chapter and therefore were developing a sound foundation on which I could build and thus grow.

I had told my bank manager I would expand and rationalize by acquisition, and in early 1976 I made my first purchase, Crowther Brothers, a small funeral business in West Bromwich. The business was in a poor state. The fleet consisted of two ancient Austin Princess limousines, and the first time we used one of them the gear stick came away in the driver's hand. The previous owner had badly miscalculated the number of funerals he had been conducting from West Bromwich, and I wondered why there seemed to be a sharp decline once I took over. Fortunately, I had bought the business partly on an earn-out basis, with half to be paid after a year, dependent on performance. In the end we agreed on a lower sum for the second payment, after he agreed he had miscalculated the original figure. This was a messy, awkward transaction, but after 126 years in the business,

Hodgson & Sons had started down the road to rationalization, and funeral directing in clusters had come to stay. We did not know it then, but the company was to change everything, including the whole profession.

Throughout 1976 and 1977, the small team at Hodgsons worked day and night to increase the number of funerals it handled, and to make sure each was carried out as efficiently as possible. By 1978 the annual number was back up to 700. I made my second acquisition, A. Hamer & Son, in Oldbury.

The next acquisition was Brookes of Brierley Hill, which had been advertised under a post box number while I was on holiday in 1979. As soon as I returned from holiday I received a telephone call from Mr Brookes, and impulsively, as was my style then, I went to see him immediately and bought the business that day, although contracts were not exchanged until I was assured and reassured concerning all financial and funeral numbers. I was learning to be very cautious and undertake proper due diligence (I had been guilty of not going far enough in this direction when buying Crowther).

I now realized that continued expansion would necessitate a strengthening of the management team, and upon recommendation from my solicitor decided to appoint his cousin Graham Hodson. I drove to Graham's home in Stafford, and told him to leave GEC and come and work for me. 'What do you get at present?' I asked him. Graham was so taken aback by my brashness that he told me, almost without hesitating, that his salary was £6,000. He staggered when I told him that in that case he was going to work for me for £5,500. I explained: 'I want to be absolutely sure that you really do want to be part of Hodgson's, because I am offering you a ride to the very top of the funeral directing business in Britain.' Hoping I was being as persuasive with Graham as I had been with the bank manager, I assured him that if he decided to throw in his lot with me he would never regret doing so. Together we would work wonders on the attitudes and standards of funeral directing. It was going to be a transformation that nobody was expecting.

Hodson was persuaded, and joined in 1979, whereupon he was put through the baptism of washing the hearses, collecting bodies, and acting as a driver/bearer. However, such a strict regime seems to have worked, as Master Hodson – then 'management trainee and apprentice extraordinaire' – went on to become a public company deputy chief executive.

It is interesting that I was ready to embark on major expansion of my business in 1979, the same year that a new Conservative Government came to power, led by a prime minister who promised to put in to effect nothing less than a revolution in government, business practices, and the attitude of the people.

In the latter part of the 1970s, the government and economy of the country sank so low that people feared it was about to go into absolute decline. Compared with its major competitors, it had been in decline for nearly thirty years. As I struggled to build my father's business, the general economic scene did in fact improve, but only slowly and with several lurches towards disaster. Inflation continued at an alarmingly high rate, and was threatening to become hyper-inflation – in 1974, wages had risen by 30% and 40% seemed to be the unions' target for 1975, as they refused to allow any curb on free collective bargaining.

In those days of strong union influence over government, Jack Jones, general secretary of the Transport and General Workers Union (TUC), a very powerful – some thought the most powerful – man in the country, realized the party was over. The so-called 'Social Contract', introduced the year before, had only been honoured in the breach by the unions. Jones recognised that something must be done to persuade the unions to treat pay claims more sensibly, otherwise hyper-inflation would result and that would be hurtful to working people whom Jones, however misguided for most of his working life genuinely wanted to help.

At roughly the same time, Jones and Harold Wilson's aide Joe Haines came up with the idea of a voluntary flat-rate policy, as Haines said, 'A fiver, everyone can understand a fiver!', which would help the poor most, and effectively meant the rich would get nothing. The government leapt on the idea, and were helped in their promotion by another sterling crisis. After much argument, the TUC general council approved a flat-rate £6-a-week policy, with zero increases for those earning more than £8,500 (£25,000 in 1992 terms).

In the short-term it worked. Inflation fell from 24.4% in 1975 to 8.3% in 1978. However, it was rough-and-ready justice, building up anomalies and grievances that exploded in the 1978 'Winter of Discontent'. As the Labour MP Philip Whitehead said in his book *The Writing on the Wall*:

> Caught between its rhetoric in opposition on the one hand, and the frustrations of its supporters on the other, Labour could not expect an ad hoc incomes policy to be credible for the course of a parliament. Wilson did not solve his economic problems. He bought time. And time, in July 1975, seemed a very scarce commodity.

A further crisis blew up in the autumn of 1976, and as sterling fell like a stone, Chancellor Denis Healey was forced to make a humiliating return from Heathrow Airport on his way to an International Monetary Fund (IMF) conference in Manila. Healey went to the Labour Party Conference at Blackpool, where the new Prime Minister, James Callaghan (Harold Wilson had resigned in the spring of 1976) had already made a blunt speech to the delegates stating that: Britain has lived too long on borrowed money, borrowed ideas. . . . For too long, perhaps ever since the war, we've postponed facing up to fundamental choices and fundamental changes in our society and our economy. . . .

> That is what I mean when I say we have been living on borrowed time. For too long this country, all of us – yes, this conference too – has been ready to settle for borrowing money abroad to maintain our standards of life, instead of grappling with the fundamental problems of British industry.

> We used to think that you could spend your way out of a recession and increase employment by cutting taxes and boosting government spending. I tell you in all candour that the option no longer exists, and that, insofar as it ever did exist, it only worked on each occasion since the war by injecting a bigger dose of inflation into the economy, followed by a higher level of unemployment as the next step. Higher inflation followed by higher unemployment – that is the history of the last twenty years.

Well said 'Sunny Jim' except he could hardly have been referring to the Labour Party when talking of cutting taxes. They have never been guilty of that. It was a speech as much for Manila as for the delegates, and with the pound in free-fall, it was very necessary. The government needed an IMF loan, and after a much publicized but nonetheless furtive visit from IMF officials, a loan was secured, but only on the basis of substantial public expenditure cuts and an agreement to continue incomes policies.

Throughout the two Labour Administrations, from February 1974 to May 1979, the tenor and rhetoric had been about the evils of the rich. Before the 1974 election, Healey talked of 'squeezing the rich until the pips squeaked'. Another Cabinet member, Anthony Wedgwood Benn, formerly Lord Stansgate, attacked both the rich and the middle class increasingly and supported every strike, official or unofficial. The TUC and its leading members came and went constantly to and from 10 Downing Street, and expostulated on the 'Nine O'clock News', 'News at Ten' and 'Panorama' on how the country should be run for the benefit of the workers. A moment of farce was reached when a union official stated dogmatically on the 'Nine O'clock News' that 'every worker should get at least the average pay rise'.

The middle classes felt they were living in an alien land and under constant attack, and the feeling got worse when Chancellor Healey, in his budget speech imposed a 95% marginal tax rate with these words.

> I believe that this type of redistribution through the tax system makes a major contribution to the health of the community as a whole – and I intend to go a great deal further before I have finished.

Patrick Hutber, the city editor of the *Sunday Telegraph* hit back in his book *The Decline and Fall of the Middle Class:*

> Now I think that, on the contrary, tax rates of this order do a grave disservice to the community. Let me, unlike Mr Healey, give my reasons. The first, which will come as no surprise after my definition of the middle class, is that they make thrift in any meaningful sense impossible. This not merely discourages independence and self-reliance, but it means that a high taxation society becomes self-perpetuating. From an economic point of view, a pound saved is a 'good' to the Government in terms of regulating consumption and, indeed, of Government finance as a pound taken in taxation. Low savings mean high taxation, high taxation means low savings. One aspect of freedom, though it may be an unfashionable aspect these days, is freedom to choose what to do with one's money, to spend it and save it according to one's own judgement rather than have the Government do all the spending and very occasionally the saving, on one's behalf.

Hutber went on to print that he felt it was wrong for everyone to be reliant on the state for everything. Finally he pointed out that high taxation discouraged the payment of high salaries. This might be thought of as a social advantage but in an increasingly international economy it meant that British companies would not attract the best people and even if it did would not give them much incentive to work hard.

While Hutber was attacking socialism and the dreadful damage brought by inflation the Tory Party ousted its leader, Edward Heath, who had put in place many of the doctrines so beloved by his opponents, the Labour Party, such as restrictions on wages, prices and dividends. In his place the Party elected a woman who, under the tutelage of Sir Keith Joseph, had grasped certain essentials of the remedy required to restore economic sanity to the country.

Immediately after the election defeat in 1974, they began to exchange a common analysis of what had gone wrong. It was, as they have both testified, a shared journey of discovery. Usefully, Sir Keith began performing this in public and without delay.

He believed that both Labour and Conservative governments since the war had believed in 'unity'. This had meant in reality that for 30 years the private sector had been forced to fight with one hand tied behind its back by government and unions. At the same time and for the same reasons, both parties, when in power, had allowed state spending to be too high, kept defunct industries artificially alive with the taxpayers' money and bought industrial peace at any price, again with the taxpayers' cash. Was it surprising that over this period we had slipped sadly behind our European competitors? And where would this total disregard for economic efficiency end?

Sir Keith then made a great discovery about himself. He had joined the Conservative Party in the early 1950s but it was not until the mid 1970s that he was converted to 'Real Economic Conservatism' and realised that previously he, like his Party, had not been Conservative at all.

Sir Keith's comments may seem just common sense now after a decade of Thatcher and the defeat of socialism in Eastern Europe. However it was a very different world then. Joseph had ruled himself out as a possible leader due to a speech made in Birmingham in early 1975, which stated that people at the bottom of the social scale were having too many children and were ill-equipped to bring them up. It smacked of racism and elitism, and when Joseph withdrew his challenge to Heath's leadership, Margaret Thatcher was able to take it up.

From February 1975 until she came to power in May 1979, Mrs Thatcher and her supporters prepared the ground for a revolution in Britain's economic attitudes. She brought clarity of thought and purpose in almost simple yet unshakeable beliefs. Tax was too high. High-rate tax collected little revenues, destroyed ambition and was a 'symbol of British socialism – the symbol of envy'. Lower rates of tax were too high. The people had a right to decide how to spend their money rather than the government do it bureaucratically for them and of course if 'earn more' really meant 'keep more' then that was incentive and we all needed that. Unless tax rates were to change across the board she could see no change from perpetual decline.

Having earned more and kept more we all – families, businesses, local and central government – needed to be good housekeepers. We must balance our budgets and exercise thrift and prudence. The power of this message, especially following decades of Labour and Conservative governments which had failed to balance budgets, should not be underestimated.

Government must set an example. Public expenditure must be controlled. Public spending should not exceed public revenue. A nation must create wealth before it spends wealth. 'You cannot look after the hard up people in Society unless you are accruing enough wealth to do so,' she told a BBC reporter in 1977, 'good intentions are not enough. You do need hard cash.' No government had a magic wand and the more the nation, or more importantly the nation's families, put into life the more they would get out. The more we expected of ourselves and the less we expected of the state the more successful both we and the state became. Whereas the converse was also true she believed. I agreed with her. This was music to the ears of businessmen, but to a certain extent – even if it was not spelled out with quite the same rigour – they had heard it before. Heath had come to power in 1970 making not dissimilar noises, only to buckle under to corporatist solutions as soon as the going got rough. Would this woman be different?

Well, we know the answer and anyone who succeeded in business in the next decade owed more than a little to the climate she created. There were to be many mistakes. There always are, but the courage she used to allow enterprise to thrive has to be applauded.

I did not know how courageous she was going to be then and I was not going to wait to find out. In 1980 I borrowed heavily to make my first big takeover, big in that it doubled the number of funerals I was handling from 1,000 to 2,000 a year, and because it took me away from my confined area of Handsworth, Birmingham, and the Black Country. Northampton is not far away – less than an hour's drive, on the motorway – but funerals were conducted differently: in Birmingham, on the way to pick up the mourners the hearse was driven behind the other cars, in Northampton it was driven in front; in Birmingham the funeral director did not stay in the church during the funeral service, in Northampton he would stay in the pew opposite the main mourner; in Birmingham the funeral director walked a funeral away, in Northampton he did not.

However, this was for the future. For the moment, I had beaten the major groups, Great Southern, Ingall's, Kenyon, and the Co-op, and had bought a company doing 1,000 funerals from one establishment. Nevertheless, I was worried. When the agents phoned to tell me I had won, my elation was considerable – but it lasted only until I put the phone down, and then I thought, 'Oh, God, I owe the bank £350,000! What am I going to do? What happens if the death rate falls? How am I going to pay it back?' It was like Hartlepool United winning the FA Cup. We had become giant killers and doubled our size at a stroke.

I had no need to worry. Bonham's was a well-established business with a proud history. It had been founded in the same year as Hodgson, 1850, by Frederick Bonham and had originally operated as carriage masters supplying carriages for the Royal Mail and for trips from Northampton Square on a Sunday. When Frederick died at the comparatively young age of 46 his wife Ann took over and it was Ann who introduced funerals, conducting them herself.

Its position in the centre of Northampton was perfect – half-way between the general hospital and the registrar. At the time I bought the firm it was run by the founder's two great grandsons, Denis and Cyril, and although the two did not get on well, they nevertheless ran an efficient funeral business. Indeed, Hodgsons was able to incorporate several of Bonham's practices into its own operations.

Its general manager, Don York, who went on to become a regional director with PHKI, remembers his early days at Bonham's, which gives an insight into funeral directing in the 1950s and 1960s. His salary was £7.50 a week, about £75 in 1991 terms, and he received an extra 2s 6d, 12.5p or about £1 in 1991 terms, for picking up bodies out of town in the country under the contract Bonham's had with the coroner. He had to buy his own uniform. During the 1950s York learned coffin-making, as Bonhams supplied coffins to other funeral directors in the area. In the villages, the funeral director was often a carpenter or blacksmith who conducted funerals part-time. There was usually a laying-out lady, who put pennies on the eyes of the deceased and tied up the mouth. The cost of a funeral in 1950, for a hearse, coffin, two cars, church service and grave was £27.10d. The average weekly wage was only £3, so my oft-quoted maxim that a funeral cost nine times the postwar working wage, whereas in the 1980s it was only three times, is correct.

With the Bonhams acquisition we had truly expanded, and the result was a 500% increase in turnover from year one to five. We were now arranging over 2,000 funerals a year from seven Midland locations. The initial growth and branching-out hurdle had been successfully jumped.

CHAPTER 4

LIFT OFF AND EXPANSION

£

Your plan has been accepted, with, no doubt, a lot more work and pain than suggested in the television advertisements for banks. You are ready to go. You know the twelve points noted earlier, and you believe you are going to be a big success. But wait a minute. There are two or three things you should know that are important. They are not really business points, but they will make a difference – for the worse if you ignore them.

SOME GENERAL DOS AND DON'TS

● **Jealousy**. Do not be jealous of anyone. Not of your competitors, and certainly not of anyone on your staff. Jealousy and hate are signs of fear. You must be more confident of your own ability than that.

● **Know your own weaknesses**. Work on them, but also get other people to help in areas where you are not too strong. Nobody is perfect. Analyse where you need help; be honest with yourself and get what you need. The success of the business is more important than massaging your ego (and the ultimate success of the business is wonderful for your ego anyway). I know this is hard to swallow, especially when you are young. It was for me, and I caused myself a lot of unnecessary work by refusing to think I was less than perfect.

● **Self-discipline**. Be harder on yourself than you are on your staff. Good leaders, especially in small units, lead by example.

● **Time-keeping**. Always be punctual. It is polite and indicates good planning.

● **Politeness**. Always be polite and cultivate good manners. You may need to be tough, you never need to behave like a pig.

- **Working environment**. John Gunn works with opera on in the background. I wrote this book to Beethoven. You choose whatever suits you and brings the best out of you.

- **Do not drink**. Alcohol and work do not mix. It is bad for you, and a bad example to set.

- **Women**. Are as good, better, and worse than men. Never judge the ability of anyone by their sex.

- **Sex**. Well, not with your staff members. My father used to say, 'Don't shit on your own doorstep', and he was right.

- **Personal guarantees**. Never, never sign them if possible, and always know what you are signing. Read everything carefully, and always ask your solicitor if you are not sure.

- **Balance sheets, etc**. Do not pretend to understand them if you do not; that goes for any documentation.

- **Sport and hobbies**. Your business must come first. If you run it around your involvement with the local cricket team, then your batting average may go up but your profits certainly will not.

- **Socialists**. When choosing your management team avoid people who make a lot of noise about being sworn socialists. Such people are often either well-intentioned, old-fashioned hypocrites or badly intentioned rather clever hypocrites. Either way they usually seem to be quite allergic to the business work ethic. This does *not* apply to reserved socialists. Indeed be wary of anyone who is too committed to anything that could distract them from the success of your business. Only the committed team wins.

- **Dazzle**. Never be too dazzled or too impressed by anyone, especially not your competitors. You may institute competitors' ideas if it is the correct action to take, having carefully thought the policy through. But imitation on the grounds of 'they're doing it therefore we must' is often a huge mistake made by small and large companies alike.

- **Family**. Talk to your wife and family about the business. Do not bore them, but involve them enough for them to share in your hopes and dreams. Let them share in your successes, as they will have to make sacrifices just like you. Your business is there for them. It is an ally, not an enemy.

46

Now, armed with the points you expected and those you did not, you are ready to grow.

GROWTH

Expanding a small business can be difficult, as it is not always easy to know when to expand internally, while keeping one eye on your market and the other on the country's economy, where often little matters like interest rates can have a serious effect on your future development. Take these factors into account, and try to know what the worst possible scenario could bring before beginning an expansion project.

CAPACITY

Plan your internal capacity levels. For example, when I first became the proprietor of Hodgson & Sons, I realized that in order to offer an excellent standard of service I would need to have one hearse, two limousines, one ambulance, one funeral director (myself), three full-time chauffeur/bearers, and one administrator. This complement of staff and capital equipment would reach an optimum performance at approximately 500 funerals per annum. Thereafter, the complement would have to be doubled, which would stand me equally in good stead until 1,000 funerals per annum was the level of operation. The same additional complement would be needed to go to 1,500, and so on.

It is most important to work this out in your own business, as you are going to need to know at what point you will have to invest further in order to meet demand and keep up standards of service, and so on. Furthermore, by having this knowledge you can plan in advance and more easily arrange the finance you will need to expand your business at the appropriate time.

CLIENTS

As the chief executive and majority shareholder of your now-growing business, you may be forgiven for thinking you are the most important person associated with it. This is quite wrong. Your *client* is the most important person, because without his support you have nothing. Lose your client – lose your business. It also is economically inefficient to market your product to new clients in order to replace the ones you have lost through incompetence.

STAFF

Your staff are also very important, because without them you will be unable to satisfy your client. In these early years, stay close to the ground floor of the business and lead the staff by example. This is motivating for them, and essential experience for you, especially in years to come when your business has grown to a much larger size and inevitably you are further removed from its day-to-day running.

Your involvement and actions during this period of your company's history are the folklore of the future. The stories will become exaggerated. One concerning myself is a classic case. On being told by the embalming staff that the snow was too deep for them to push the wheel-biers through from the mortuary to the main funeral home so the coffins could be presented in private chapels for viewing, I came down from my office, placed one coffin on a bier, pushed it through the snow, up the ramp, and into the funeral home. A posse of embalming staff trotted behind me, apologizing profusely and saying they could manage. A decade later, the story is that, on being told the same information, I arrived in the mortuary, picked up two coffins, placed one under each arm, and strode across the yard, transporting both the coffins and their occupants safely and successfully through the snow.

TECHNOLOGY

Do not be afraid to use new technology where applicable, especially computers. However, avoid unnecessary gadgetry, which you may be tempted to acquire as an ego-booster rather than to fulfil a useful function. Also, your growing business will become a target for salesmen wishing to sell their technology, and, according to them, it is only with their technology that you will beat the opposition. Do not be frightened to invest and use new technology, but first assure yourself that it is an essential investment. The acid test is how such an investment improves your company's performance, both in the short- and long-term. Hodgson & Sons was slow to accept computer technology, which would have been labour-saving if taken on at an earlier stage. This was a mistake.

When your business starts to grow and you feel more confident about the future, do not get distracted. It is essential that you keep pumping both time and money back into the business; it is at this stage that most businessmen become content and the impetus is lost.

BRANCHING OUT

You have seen your business through its infant stage. It now has a firm base, and the core business is successful. You are now keen to branch out. If possible, avoid diversification. First, because you know about the business you are in, this does *not* mean you know how to be successful in another; second, you would probably lose the advantages of economies of scale; and third, if at a later date you wish to float the company, the stock-market by and large dislikes small companies that mess about in many unrelated fields.

For example, when I floated Hodgson Holdings plc on the USM in 1986 it was a funeral directing company, pure and simple. In those days, funeral directing was considered a jokey little cottage industry, and hardly the sort of business associated with flotation. The City, however, quickly under-stood what Hodgson Holdings did, why it did it, and that it did it more professionally and profitably than its competitors. As a result, the flotation was successful and the institutions proved to be keen to follow the stock, with its price rocketing from 85p on flotation in 1986 to £2.96 within a year. If Hodgson Holdings had undertaken many different activities, and at one time we seriously considered purchasing my wife's boutique business, the company would have appeared less attractive to the City as its message would have been less clear.

Where diversification is either desirable or unavoidable this should be a synergy of activity if possible and hopefully common factors like plant, land, labour and even management will be shared by the separate businesses.

If branching out means literally opening new branches, always ask yourself the following questions:

- What is the current market size of the new proposed area?

- What is the potential market size of the proposed area?

- Is it too close to the present location, or could it be nearer?

- What is the extent of the existing competition in the new area?

- What are the characteristics of the new proposed area; could any local traditions have either a good or bad effect on trade?

- What is the religious, racial and financial status of the proposed area? This is asked purely from a business point of view: you must understand where the market is coming from in your new area.

- Should your business develop towards intense local market share, or a wider area with a lower percentage?

- What about 1992? At the time of writing, I am making a programme with the BBC about whether British businessmen are prepared for 1992. The unfortunate evidence is they are not. Most British businessmen have failed even to think of Europe in 1992, and if they have they are thinking of how they might protect their home market. Very few have considered that just over a very small body of water there is a market that has more than 340 million potential clients. Ask yourself: will you open your fiftieth branch in Skegness and not in Paris? If so, why?

Ninety percent of German businessmen speak English, whereas only seven percent of British businessmen speak German. Is this good enough? Do you speak another language? If not should you be learning?

• Expand with courage, but not before you have thought through the options and made a plan.

REPORTING

Now that you are branching out, the need to have accurate data from other areas of your business becomes essential. You must take consistent reports. My view is that wherever possible a report should be multifunctional. Preferably any reports which are compiled by individuals should prove to be as valuable to that person as to the recipient.

Within the branch network it is vital that activity is well planned and the results compiled. Good planning ensures maximum time utilisation and provides the foundation upon which sales can be built. Analysis of results helps identify problem areas, provides market feedback and assists the better targeting of new business approaches

In addition it can assist the compiler by giving him a guide to the type of activity that he should be engaged in on a regular basis as well as giving him up to the minute information on his branch.

From the company's point of view it provides a control mechanism with which to regulate the whole network at all levels.

You should put in place planning devices which are designed to either co-ordinate or focus activity; the master planner and from these much of the 'report' information should be drawn.

A series of reports should then be introduced; the weekly marketing analysis, the weekly Branch Manager report, the Area Manager visit report, etc., etc. to include any information that you need in order to efficiently run the business on a day by day basis.

DELEGATION

As your company grows, you must learn to delegate. When and by how much is not easy to judge. The key to good management is delegation; the key to good delegation is management. When to delegate must be debatable, but to whom is not: you can only delegate to a person with management ability. You must not delegate to anyone who does not have management ability, even if they are well versed in your business. When to delegate depends on the growth of the company, and therefore the efficient use of your time; it also depends on the readiness of the person you are delegating to. Good delegation is not just giving something you used to do to someone else, but showing them, doing it with them, and giving them team confidence. Good delegation is like teaching your son or daughter to ride a bicycle: the child thinks you still have your hand on the seat, when actually you let go 200 yards previously.

MIDDLE MANAGEMENT

Initially, it is not a bad idea to promote personnel internally, as you know the people and they have been part of your dream and therefore deserve consideration. Obviously they must be capable. If they are good enough, their promotion will not only be motivating to them, but will encourage others, and all your staff will see that they can share in your success.

Do not, however, get into the habit of only promoting from within the company. You need good middle management, and *now* you can afford it. If you only promote internally, sooner or later you will suck good people off the ground floor into areas of management where they are not so capable, having denuded yourself of their capabilities at lower management levels. It is easier to teach outside people with management ability the culture of your profession or trade than it is to teach people with a knowledge of your trade management ability.

TRAINING

As your company grows, the question of training becomes more relevant. Train from the top-down and not from the bottom-up. This is essential for two reasons: firstly, untrained management will quickly wreck well-trained workers, laying to waste your investment in training the workers in the first place; secondly, management is suspicious of and negative about training schemes that teach subordinates things they have not been taught themselves.

Good training can be invaluable in motivating staff, improving their performance and potential, and giving management a means of talking to staff. Management/staff communication gets harder as a company grows, and the old 'jungle telegraph' word-of-mouth becomes ineffective.

It is essential that middle management is both capable and motivated, because it is through them that you are going to reach every nook and cranny in your company to get the best possible performance from each member of staff. Your middle management will be motivated by:

- A belief in you, the company, the product, and the future; the dream that he or she is going to have a better tomorrow because of his or her involvement in your company and your dream today.

• Present and future money prospects. The theory of poor money today but better prospects tomorrow will only work over the short term. A good man or woman should be on good pay today.

• A higher level of job satisfaction so that he or she does not only respect you and your company, but their own role as well.

• Fun. Yes, fun. It may be hard work being in your team, but it is also fun.

• A title with some status is not only motivating to the holder, but also to junior management, who dream of holding it themselves.

ACCOUNTABILITY

Middle management must always be seen to have status and authority in the area of the company for which they are responsible. Senior management must always be mindful not to override or publicly belittle middle management. It should guide them, and then leave them to take over in the knowledge that they will be held accountable.

Middle management will be at its most effective in the beginning, when the company is still fairly small and they are still close to you. As the company grows, they will become more distant and will develop their own self-protection systems and characteristics. *Their natural loyalty to the company will be directed to themselves*; some of the members may feel insecure, while others take advantage of the company size to freewheel.

I was once told by Owen Oyston, the socialist philanthropist and owner of Piccadilly Radio that middle management is both expensive and unnecessary. I agreed with the first point, but not the second. At the time Hodgson Holdings plc was only half of its eventual size and its middle management was performing extremely well. Two years later as chief executive of PHKI I was more ready to agree with the entirety of his statement. In the future, the advancement of computers and franchising may largely destroy the need for middle management in huge areas of commerce and industry.

As I moved further on the acquisition trail, I operated a system of checks to make sure my growing empire functioned efficiently, and therefore profitably. Competition was encouraged, with trophies for the best-kept funeral home, etc., and awards for 'manager of the year' presented at the company's annual conference. Every afternoon, and most days on into the evening, the regional managers reported to me on the day's happenings.

Managers were put on a bonus system, and mishaps such as damage to a hearse were deducted from the bonus. A further check was kept through customers filling in 'satisfaction' forms, giving their comments on a funeral. I also carried out spot-checks, arriving at a funeral home with a 40-point checklist, ranging from missing lavatory paper, to wasting gas and electricity. As the company grew this became a function of middle management.

Middle management is there to organize the company locally, guide the staff, and ensure that standards of service are maintained. It also keeps information flowing up and down the company, and may include future senior executives. Middle management must be motivated, positive, and have almost a religious zeal if the company is to succeed.

You must be prepared to stand by them and back them when they are right, especially in the inevitable battles they will have with your growing bureaucratic head office accounts department. For all *their* failings, middle management usually remembers the client must come first. Inhouse accountants tend to think clients pay for, and other staff are employed for, their benefit. Have as few inhouse accountants as possible. They earn no money, save little, and cost a lot.

Middle management, therefore, is either a *bloody* group who screw up the message from you to the ground floor, or the company's future senior management, or both. When they are good they are very, very good, and when they are bad, they are awful. You must get this part of the company's structure right, and you must constantly review it. Ignore middle management at your peril, and never have too much of it.

DISMISSAL

From time to time you may have to fire someone. Nobody likes firing, but it has to be done.

First, check your legal position. If you employ less than twenty people, then you can terminate an employee's contract within two years of their starting with you. If you employ more than 20, then the same is true within the first year. After that, you should give a verbal warning, confirmed in writing, followed by two written warnings; if all of this occurs within the same twelve months, you may fire the offending individual at the time of his next offence.

Certain actions of a serious nature can allow you to dismiss a person without warnings. Always consult your solicitor. Other points to note:

- Generally, do not give second chances.

- Do not demote as some form of compromise.

- Do not put off the decision or the action.

- Do not do it when you are in a temper.

- Be *totally* sure of your facts, and never act on hearsay – you may be firing the wrong person.

- If possible, have a witness present.

- If the person works for you directly, always tell them yourself and never get anyone else to handle it; your staff will think you cowardly if you delegate such an action.

PERSONAL ORGANIZATION

Things will have changed a lot from the early days. The company's growth will have altered your working day considerably. Instead of running the shop or office, your time is now spent planning the future and orchestrating the management.

It is as essential as ever that you manage your time well. If you have too much time on your hands, then you have either delegated too quickly or have insufficient capital, interest, or courage to go for the next leap forward. The guy in the pub who claims over a long lunch break that he is a great manager because 'the place runs wonderfully without me' is a fool and will go nowhere. Who owns the business? Who draws the largest salary? And therefore who should work the hardest? – You.

It is important that you consider the following:

- Organize your day/week/month around things that must be dealt with daily, weekly, or monthly. Talk to your line of management daily, and have minuted meetings with them monthly.

- Keep a diary in which everything that you and your team should do is written. Write the initial of the team member who is responsible against each item. Tick items off through the course of the day as you deal with them yourself or speak to the team member about them. At the end of the day, move all items that are continuous or unfinished forward to a future sensible date. Do this as a discipline each night before you leave, whatever the time or how short of it you are. This way, nothing gets forgotten. Ensure your management at all levels does the same.

- Communicate everything clearly, and by what date you expect the task to be finished or a report to be received. Having moved the item forward in the diary and waited for the date to arrive, do not repeat the request but ask for a result. Repeating the request suggests you did not expect management to achieve what had been agreed. Ask for the result, and be displeased if it is unsatisfactory without just reason.

- Listen to what people have to say and be objective. However remember you are the boss and therefore will have to take decisions. Having listened to others always remain your own man.

- Have an excellent secretary/PA. They will be able to organize and deal with hundreds of things each week which would have taken you hours. I was very lucky to have several in my fifteen years at Hodgson. Indeed the first three all went on to senior positions in the company. I had only one poor one whose name I will not write but gosh what a difference he made – life was a complete mess.

- Learn to discern the difference between an external appointment that could do your company good, and one where all the business gain will be with the other guy. Question the validity of an appointment, and certainly do not attend just because someone is buying you a good lunch.

- It has been written that you should never receive a phone call – in other words, tell your secretary to block everything and say you will call back. This is nonsense. If everybody adopted this attitude no business would ever get done as nobody would ever be receiving anybody else's calls. There are times to accept a call and times not to. Do not accept a phone call if:

– you are uncertain of the caller or the subject;

– you want someone else in the organization to deal with it, so you remain one place removed;

– you have not worked out what you want to say;
– it could be important and you do not feel in top form – give yourself time and call back;

– the caller is a nuisance or just not important enough for you to deal with;

– you wish to create the right impression;

– you wish to heighten tension during an important deal – only do this if you know what you are doing;

– you are in an important meeting;

– you are working on something urgent.

Otherwise, *accept* the call. To do otherwise is time-consuming and expensive as every conversation will be on your bill if you insist on calling everyone back.

FUNDING THE EXPANSION

Your business is now quite large, and most likely to get it there you have had to raise money from your bankers on several occasions. Each time you have borrowed, your house and your shirt have been promised to the bank. As your business has continued to expand, you have paid them back before going through the same exercise.

Now that you have grown, examine the interest charges you have paid to the bank, as well as your turnover-related bank charges. These should be negotiated down, and a lot of the personal security you have put forward returned to you. The bank – and these things depend very much on the attitude of the manager – may well agree. On the other hand, it may not.

At this point you must ask yourself, 'Have I outgrown this bank?' By this I do not mean has your company outgrown the size of the bank you are using, but you may well have outgrown their perception of you. This is what is known as the Jesus of Nazareth theory: Jesus was considered the son of God, except in Nazareth, where he was just the carpenter's son. The inhabitants of Nazareth, who had known him as a little boy, were horrified by his suggestion that he was the Messiah. Your bank, and in particular your bank manager, may have the same attitude towards you.

If your bank does not agree to have a serious look at lowering your bank charges and interest rate, then do not be frightened to visit several other banks to see what they will offer. Do this even if you wish to stay with your current bank, as some of the rates quoted by the opposition may provide you with a pleasant stick with which to beat your bank.

As a growing and secure company, you come across an acquisition that is important to your future growth. For you, this is a quantum leap. As ever, make a plan, and check it. You must be sure you are right, and that your heart is not ruling your head in the excitement of the moment. Is it really bank borrowings you want? It may be better to consider venture capital. But how will you know?

For one thing, you may be well extended at the bank and therefore unable to borrow more. Alternatively, you may feel (and your accountant and bank manager may agree on this) that the acquisition you are proposing is less attractive if it incurs extra gearing cost. The time may thus be right to take on a private equity investor who will help you to make the quantum-leap acquisition, or, alternatively, to talk to a venture capital company with the same thing in mind.

VENTURE CAPITAL

A venture capital proposition may work something along the following lines:

In exchange for the agreed amount of cash, the venture capital company will take an agreed number of cumulative, convertible, redeemable preference shares. Such preference shares would carry a coupon (dividend), and be convertible before a certain date, usually triggered by a flotation on the stock-market into ordinary shares, or alternatively, convertible into loan stock, which would also have a coupon and eventually become repayable. This arrangement means that the venture capital bank has an immediate income on its investment, with the prospect of the investment converting into ordinaries and making a lot of money at the time of the flotation. Alternatively, if things do not go so well it can convert them into loan stock, thus providing an exit route.

It all sounds very cosy for *them*, but how does it benefit *you*? By having the venture company on board, you have been able to do a mega-deal *that* may never have been possible, or certainly not possible for years to come. Your company, because of their involvement, now has a lot more clout with your joint stock bank, and as a result you can look forward to continued expansion, if this is the prudent thing to do.

Don't forget that in the event that the preference shares convert into ordinary shares this will dilute your share holding. To what extent obviously depends on the deal struck at the time of the negotiation with the venture capital company. However you must take this mentally on board before you do the deal as being unhappy with the idea at the time of conversion is no good as it is too late.

I allowed a venture capital company to invest in Hodgson & Sons Ltd in under one year prior to our flotation. Although they made a tremendous amount of money out of the subsequent flotation, I never complained or was resentful as without their investment capital at the time when it was needed the company would not have had such a smooth and expanding run-in to its 1986 flotation. Equally, in 1989 I had no regrets about Hodgson Holdings plc issuing unquoted preference shares to John Gunn's B&C Ventures as although the coupon was higher than the then quoted preference stock, it was thanks to B&C's investment of £15 million that (a) 'Dignity in Destiny' was launched and (b) a damaging rights issue (due to the bear market) was avoided.

Do not forget two things:

Firstly, if you are seriously considering taking on other equity partners such as a venture capital company, look right down the road to where it all ends: if you have a vision of yourself as the head of an expanding public company, having made a fortune at the time of flotation, then you may be in good company; if you are not so happy with this picture, then think long and hard before entering this course of action. You don't necessarily have to float because of the involvement of venture capital, but you do have to keep expanding.

Secondly, on no account be overawed by the guys from the venture capital bank. They will use many more technical terms than your high street bank manager, and they will appear more intelligent, which they probably are. They will have refined accents and appear to be better educated. Remember, however, that everything is negotiable: the coupon is negotiable, the amount of money being invested is negotiable, the conversion windows are negotiable, the percentage this would give them once they converted to ordinaries is negotiable and so on. Nothing is sacred and they will need you as much as you need them.

EQUITY PARTNERS

An equity partner as an alternative to a venture capital group, perhaps from a similar and even the same industry in Europe or the United States, may be the perfect answer as they may well take a stake in ordinary shares, with no current coupon, and at the same time bring experience and even clients to the party. However the potential downside of having such an equity partner early on is the giving away of shares cheaply that could be very valuable in years to come. You could be getting undressed before it is time to go to bed. Therefore the long-term loss may well be greater than the short-term gain of no gearing or coupon cost.

If your company and its expansion plans are excellent then gearing, venture capital and equity partners will be available to you – choosing which one suits you is then your job.

Whatever course of action you take, get a financial adviser who knows what he or she is talking about in what will be a new field to you. Moreover, make sure you understand the implications of the advice given.

You and your financial adviser must sit down before negotiations and know exactly where you want to be when negotiations end. Funding your expansion correctly is as important as the expansion itself. If you believe the deal is right, be brave enough to fight for it and to do it, and if you do not get what you want, be brave enough to walk away.

CHAPTER 5

PUBLIC PERSUASION

The general financial climate in Britain from 1980 to 1982 was the worst since the War, certainly in terms of corporate failures and rising unemployment. Margaret Thatcher came to power promising changes, and was determined to see them through. Tight monetary policies, allied with another sharp hike in the price of oil following the overthrow of the Shah of Iran – which in turn brought a sharp rise in the value of the pound, viewed as a petro-currency due to North Sea oil – created the most difficult trading conditions British companies had experienced since the 1930s. ICI, generally viewed as the bell-wether of British manufacturing industry, cut its dividend and Sir Terence Becket, the Director General of the CBI promised the government a 'bare-knuckle fight' saying at the CBI conference: 'We've got to have a lower pound – we've got to have lower interest rates.'

The Prime Minister remained firm and declared on the day unemployment passed the two million mark, 'I've been trying to say to people for a very long time: if you pay yourself more for producing less, you'll be in trouble.'

Mrs Thatcher's one serious mistake in the early years of her leadership was to promise to implement the Clegg Commission's recommendations. The Clegg Commission had been set up – in the classic corporatist style of the 1960s and 1970s – to appease the public-sector unions after the 1978 'Winter of Discontent', which had been the unions' answer to the Labour Government's incomes policy. Mrs Thatcher knew the Clegg recommendations would be inflationary, but she had not come this close to power to risk it by alienating anyone who might vote Tory. It meant 20% wage inflation, which, ministers thought gave every justification for going back on the promise. However, the recommendations were honoured. As cabinet minister John Biffen said, 'It would have been unthinkable . . .to cast aside . . .that which you had underwritten for the purpose of winning votes.' Cecil Parkinson correctly concluded, 'It was a mistake to endorse Clegg in the run-up to the election. . . . There's always this pressure to recognise the problems of the special interest group, and we did, and we gave the commitment which turned out to be a very, very expensive one.'

Heavy wage inflation allied to the near doubling of VAT in the first budget of the new administration, meant that within weeks inflation soared again to an average 13.13% in 1979, 18.1% in 1980 and 11.9% in 1981. Thereafter it fell to under 10.5% in time for the general election of 1983, aided by the overvalued pound and moderate wage settlements, induced by an unemployment level not seen since the 1930s.

The result of all this – combined with a very tough attitude towards the unions and strikes, epitomized by the government's approach to a national strike in the steel industry that they were determined to win whatever the cost – was that by the end of 1981 the government's and Margaret Thatcher's popularity fell to new depths. But Thatcher pressed on, and although she had invited people from the whole spectrum of the Party into her Cabinet, she took little notice of what many of them said. She was not going to 'waste time having any internal arguments'.

At the depths of the recession, and with unemployment still climbing sharply, she strongly supported Sir Geoffrey Howe's spring 1981 budget, which intensified the squeeze on both companies and the consumer. Initially, Howe had been against any such budget, and even the Treasury felt that some relaxation of monetary policy was possible. However, Mrs Thatcher's two extra-parliamentary advisers, Sir John Hoskyns, and Alan Walters, a former professor at Birmingham University and the London School of Economics did not. Walters had established his monetarist principles long before the phrase was heard in political circles. (Indeed he had predicted the inflation of 1974 as early as 1972 analysing the explosion of credit in that year in the Barber boom.)

Hoskyns and Walters helped to stiffen Thatcher's resolve in the early months of 1981. To them it was a matter of credibility. The government had to show everyone once and for all that they were not going to move forward 'with enormous insupportable borrowings'. It had to convince the financial markets that it would get inflation down. Walters pressed for £4,000 billion to come out of the public sector borrowing requirement. Chancellor Howe resisted long and hard. Thatcher knew Walters was right but then it was she and Howe and not Walters who had to sell this tough line in the House of Commons. Walters at one point doubted if Thatcher could see it through and prepared himself for resignation. However Thatcher stood firm and as a result Howe feared for his career and in the end came up with a package worth £3,500 million which Walters said was enough to do the trick, and the key budget of the Thatcher years and perhaps one of the most significant this century went ahead.

The budget produced forecasts of falling output of a further 1% while unemployment would soar to perhaps 3 million. Thatcher believed this was the price a realistic and, in the future, prosperous Britain would have to pay. She also feared the sack as she could see many faint hearts among the Tory 'wets'. But it worked. The financial markets saw that here was a Prime Minister who stuck to her guns, and applauded her toughness and resolution. As many predicted the U-turn that tough-talking governments of both parties had indulged in since the War, Thatcher went to the party Conference and told them: 'You may turn if you want to, the lady's not for turning.'

If the financial markets and international bankers were applauding Mrs Thatcher, the British public – which was at worst out of a job, and at best subjected to a severe squeeze on its standard of living – was sitting on its hands. Matters were getting somewhat desperate in the winter of 1981–2, when out of the South Atlantic appeared a group of Argentine soldiers who landed first on the island of South Georgia, and then, more seriously, on the Falkland Islands. as everyone reached for their atlases, Mrs Thatcher decided British sovereignty had been violated and the Argentinians must be removed, if necessary by force.

Our leader was courageous, our armed forces professional and, above all, we looked a winner. It was a turning point for Mrs Thatcher. Her ratings in the opinion polls soared, and as the economy showed signs of revival, she was able to go to the country and request a second term in office in order to carry on the revolution she had begun.

The stock-market, sensing political and economic recovery, and helped by Wall Street's rapid rise from a Dow Jones low of 600 in August 1982, started to move up. On both sides of the Atlantic and throughout the world the great 1980s boom had begun. Fuelling it was the decline in the price of oil – after reaching $40 a barrel in 1979 it was to fall to under $10 in 1986 – and the decline in the price of other commodities. None of this helped the Third World, but it certainly allowed the industrialized countries to enjoy several years of strong non-inflationary growth. Rapid advances in technology also provided plenty of new gadgets for the industrial countries first to produce and then to consume.

In Britain, those companies that had survived the severe recession of the early 1980s were leaner and fitter, and the leanest and fittest began to gobble up those that had survived but were reeling. A takeover boom developed on the market, which further boosted share prices, in turn providing the predators with expensive paper to boost their takeover prospects, and creating a virtuous – though to some vicious – spiral of escalating prices and financial assets.

For growing businesses like Hodgson, the climate was ideal for cashing in. Acquisitions were being made in the early 1980s, but partly with retained earnings and partly with bank borrowings. Inevitably, this process was slow, and a stock-market quotation opened the prospect of faster expansion.

Nevertheless, I was nervous. I realized that if there was going to be a bear market – which I believed there could be because there had been several years of a bull market – or if Mrs Thatcher were to lose the election, it was going to be jolly hard to set my company under way on the market. Moreover we were not sure if we could get the company on to the Unlisted Securities Market (USM) anyway as it was a funeral company; there only had been one such flotation previously, and that had been Kenyon's rather hammy and restricted effort in 1983. Ingall's was a fully listed public company, but had floated as an engineering company, only moving into funeral directing later. There was no evidence that in these heady times of high-profile flotations, which brought masses of publicity, there was going to be any room in the market for a funeral company.

I remember being very coy about it all and saying we would do only one press interview. This turned out to be with John Jay of the *Sunday Telegraph* and as he treated it seriously we were not as nervous thereafter.

The actual preparations for the flotation were put in hand with Capel Cure Myers CCM. Nevertheless a flotation would not be easy. Hodgson was making profits of only £200,000 and enjoyed a nil net asset value, thanks to the goodwill element in the balance sheet from their acquisitions. Intensive work would be necessary. One of the first requirements was a new bank. We switched from Midland to Lloyds – we had outgrown Midland's perception of us – in order to continue our acquisition program. However by the end of 1985, as we acquired A. V. Band of Worcester even Lloyds were a little anxious about their commitment, and were keen for either a flotation or the raising of some long-term capital flow from a financial institution. As a result, I approached Sharp Unquoted Midland Investment Trust Limited (SUMIT), part of the Albert E. Sharpe group, who took an 8.3% stake for £396,000 and also subscribed £350,000 for a combination of convertible preference shares and loan stock.

To oversee their investment they put one of their people on the Hodgson board. This stabilized the financial situation at the end of 1985, but was not sufficient for my ambitions. I could see the possibilities of growth through acquisition, and only a public company would provide the vehicle for me to advance rapidly. In spite of my fears of a stock-market bear-phase – one did come, of course, in October 1987 – the conditions at the end of 1985 were perfect. Takeovers were being announced almost every day and on a bigger and bigger scale. In the City, many banks and stockbrokers were selling themselves to larger, often overseas, financial institutions as they prepared for their own revolution known as the 'Big Bang'.

As with the unions and many companies, the City of London had become a nice cosy cartel. Like them, it needed shaking up to cope with the international competition lining up in the 1980s. The London Stock Exchange showed no inclination to mend its ways until Sir Gordon Borrie, the head of the Office of Fair Trading (OFT), threatened to take them to court under the Restrictive Trade Practices Act. As the knives came out, Cecil Parkinson, at that time minister at the Department of Trade and Industry, did a deal with the Stock Exchange. The system of fixed commissions would be scrapped, not gradually but all at once. Furthermore, all dealings would be computerized. This brave new world for the City led to a period of frenetic activity, as financial conglomerates were constructed hastily and often foolishly. It all added to excitement in the market, and prices rose continuously. The general business background was also helpful as company profits and dividends increased steadily. The conditions for flotation were ideal.

Once the decision was made, I wanted it done quickly. We motored from February to May 1986. We worked twenty hours a day. I had some appalling sessions with drafting people which made me completely allergic to them and I have remained so ever since. By May the work was done. All that was left was to decide the flotation price, and to organize the coverage in the press necessary to launch a company successfully. Nevill Boyd Mansell in the *Birmingham Post* was very supportive:

Just a year after Ingall was taken over by the House of Fraser, Birmingham is going to have another publicly quoted undertaker. Hodgson Holdings, still based in Handsworth where it was founded in 1850, is bringing 32 per cent of its shares to the Unlisted Securities Market this week, through a placing arranged by the ANZ Merchant Bank (owners of CCM).

The plan is to raise about £3 million for the company to enable it to continue a policy of expanding by buying up what it perceives as less-efficient funeral businesses – a policy which has carried its own profits from £113,000 in 1981 to £484,000 last year and £442,000 for the six months to April. Existing shareholders will collect £1.2 million, among them the Sharp Unlisted Midlands Investment Trust, which will be left with 8.5 per cent of the enlarged equity after selling 3 per cent.

But why invest in him? Well, his market is never going to collapse. You could also argue that he is the funeral industry Lord Hanson. The ANZ Bank believes that his shares are worth, say 14 years' earnings in the present stock market, linked with a yield of under 4 per cent.

Now Mr Hodgson says he can buy another undertaker for one year's turnover or five or six years' earnings. From day one, those earnings will be reflected in his own much more highly rated shares. And he has a very specific formula for increasing them. ('We go in with a 155-point hit list when we acquire a company.')

In all, he has 24 offices, none so far in London or the South, which expect to do 5,600 funerals a year, about one per cent of the total in England and Wales. The nearest he comes to a local monopoly is with something like 60 per cent in Northampton and 20 per cent in Northamptonshire. The Co-op has about 25 per cent overall and House of Fraser 5 per cent.

Much of the rest of the work is done by 2,000 small family businesses. Mr Hodgson believes many of them are hopelessly badly managed – and ripe to be taken over during the next ten years.

The Times also made reference to Lord Hanson – generally accepted as one of Britain's most efficient businessmen – saying: 'Mr Hodgson, 36, borrowed a leaf out of the book of Lord Hanson in employing economies of scale in the funeral business.'

At this stage, *The Times* did not make any recommendation about whether its readers should buy the shares; nor did the *Financial Times* or the *Guardian*. The *Daily Mail*, referring to me as the funeral whizz-kid, said 'The shares should do well.' The *Investors Chronicle* after quoting one of my favourite quips of the day – death is to the twentieth century what sex was to the Victorians, an enigma – described the shares, with a prospective price/earnings ratio of 14 and a yield of 3.6%, as 'fair value'.

In the event, the shares, launched at 85p on 16 June 1986, soon moved to a premium of 7p. I wasted no time in using my new financial muscle to make a flurry of takeovers through the autumn of 1986 and the early months of 1987. By March 1987, on the back of this activity and a strong bull market for all shares, our shares rose from a launch price of 85p to 185p – fair value indeed!

In its review of the funeral directors on the market the USM magazine noted that the funeral sector was beginning to attract attention. The name of the game in a static market was acquisition, but as the many small private enterprises willing to sell could usually be bought for an exit multiple of six times, the possibilities for earnings enhancement for the quoted groups on much higher price earnings multiples were enormous. And of course, the more acquisitions they did, the better the story became. They were in the classic bull market virtuous circle. Furthermore, the scope for improving the performance of the companies acquired was also enormous.

There are fairly straightforward operating efficiencies and systems and economies of scale that can improve the returns of an acquired business. Essentially, funeral directing is a business whereby big, efficient operators squeeze out smaller competitors who cannot achieve the same economies of scale and therefore maintain the same margins.

The review went on to say that Hodgson's 'acquisition-led tenfold increases in funerals conducted per annum and consistent profit growth suggest it is a well-managed concern with a sound future', while Kenyon, though well-managed, had enjoyed only modest growth and Great Southern's unfriendly stake (nearly 19%) provided the basis for a potential bid, 'suggesting that this stake is for the speculative investor'. In view of later events this was a canny prediction.

Shortly after the flotation I received a surprise accolade by being voted one of the 'Top 40 Under 40' businessmen in the country by the new glossy magazine *Business*. However as one lawyer who made the list said, 'I wonder if this will ruin my career?' If that lawyer was Anthony Salz of Freshfields his career was certainly not helped by his close association with the Guinness company while it was buying Distillers. And some did fall by the way before the 1990s arrived: Olivier Roux, damaged by his close association with Guinness while on secondment from the American consultants, Bain & Co.; John Ashcroft, the chairman and chief executive of Coloroll, which went into receivership in early 1990; and Roger Felber, whose Parkfield Group also went into receivership in early 1990, another victim of heavy borrowings in an era of high interest rates.

Others hit hard times, staggered, and recovered their poise: Alan Sugar, whose Amstrad enjoyed phenomenal growth in the early and mid–1980s found life tougher in 1988 and 1989, but was not one to give in easily, and by 1990 had put his company back on a growth tack; Michael Green of Carlton Communications also found it difficult to fulfil some of the heady market expectations, and in 1990 the company's shares suffered a series of 'bear raids' that sent them reeling to one-third of their peak value.

Nevertheless, the underlying strength of his company had steadied the situation by the end of 1990 and he was to achieve his ambition of gaining the Thames Television franchise in 1991.

The remainder, including Richard Branson, Gerald Ratner, Bruce Oldfield, and Nigel Rudd, continued to prosper, and by the beginning of 1991 were busy seeing their companies through the worst recession since the early 1980s. Whether they emerge as Britain's leaders remains to be seen. Gerald in particular may be a little sadder and a little wiser after his experiences in 1991.

The 'Top 40 Under 40' came as a complete surprise. I never even read *Business* magazine, and I certainly did not expect to be elected and I really have to say in all honesty I do not think I ever should have been because there were an awful lot of people at that time at the sharp end of industry outside London who had done amazing things during the early 1980s recession at relatively young ages. It was London and media orientated. We all had to autograph photos and go to the presentation, cluster around a piano with Richard Branson playing and sing something stupid for 'News at Ten' like 'Hi ho, hi ho, it's off to work we go'. For 1986 it was very neat – business entrepreneur replaces soccer star as bedfellow of rock star as sex symbol.

The fact that I was included in the list did no harm at all, especially in the City where a high profile kept the Hodgson share price bubbling, thereby making acquisitions easier. And the acquisitions came at a rapid rate. By the end of 1986 the company was handling 50% more funerals than it had when it floated in June. Boyd Mansell in the *Birmingham Post* was happy to continue his support: 'Yesterday he (Howard) had to deliver, in hard figures for the year to October. Sure enough, his £840,000 profit was 15% ahead of his forecast in June and 65% of his final year as a private company.'

It was not surprising that the *Birmingham Post* was a fan of the local boy made good. What was more gratifying was praise from the *Financial Times* which reported, in January 1987:

> The death rate may be static but that presents few problems for the expansion of Hodgson. A few years ago undertaking was very much a family affair, but as the amount of money spent on funerals has declined more companies have come up for sale. Hodgson and others have therefore been able to buy up competitors and then introduce classic economy of scale policies. This is one reason for pre-tax margins in 1986 of about 30%. Another has been the company's growing success in selling ancillaries such as flowers and memorials. The coming year should see profits in the £1.2 million range, putting the shares of 196p on a prospective p/e of 22. The high ratings will put some investors off but the

shares, which traded at just 85p when the company was floated 1st June, represent reasonable value for those prepared to take the long view.

Hodgson Holdings was one of the stars of the Unlisted Securities Market (USM). Between 1981–7, aided by a burgeoning bull market, more than 500 companies were floated on the USM. Most had a relatively humdrum reception; some experienced difficult launches where many shares were left with the underwriters and the shares opened at a discount. These faltering starters included Marina Developments, M6 Cash and Carry, Wooltons Betterware and the eponymous American cookie company run by Mrs Fields (this last company disconcertingly just before Hodgson's float). On the other hand Anglia Secure Homes, the Shield Group, Miller and Santhouse, Northumbrian Fine Foods and Hodgson Holdings were great successes. In March 1987 I won the 'Entrepreneur of the Year' Award at the USM Awards dinner. My view of these awards was sceptical.

Journalists can be lazy – within a few months I was in the *Sunday Times* colour supplement, and a few weeks after that came 'Maggie's Dozen of the Decade', also in the *Sunday Times*. Then it was 'Howard's Way', the BBC2 television documentary, and thirty-five more television appearances in four years. It all feeds itself.

This welter of publicity was all well organized and orchestrated by Simon Preston Associates, the PR company introduced to me by the stockbroker, Capel Cure Myers, before the flotation. Run by the charming, experienced and urbane Simon Preston, his company won the Hodgson account in competition with Dorland Business Communications, also introduced by Capel Cure Myers, because, in Preston's view, he asked the more relevant questions. In mine, he looked more like a funeral director.

Shortly after the favourable press reception to its first results as a public company, Hodgson launched its tenth bid since going public for a Doncaster firm called J. Steadman. And the acquisition trail continued. To further it, I gathered round me a young team of like-minded individuals: Steven Heathcote, who had been at preparatory school with me, joined the board just before flotation and stayed on as company secretary; Simon Ramshaw, a solicitor with Edge & Ellison, had been acting for SUMIT when I was looking for an institutional investor in 1985. At the time Hodgson needed to engage a more substantial legal firm with greater expertise and, impressed with Ramshaw, began to use the services of Edge & Ellison. Ramshaw built at Edge's an acquisition team; and Hodgson kept it busy for the following three years. Hodgson engaged a new finance director, Ron Middleton, who also by sheer coincidence (Birmingham is only a village) had been at preparatory school with me. Like Heathcote, Middleton guessed I was 'going places', and decided to swap the safe, but perhaps slightly claustrophobic, life as a partner in his firm of accountants for life in the potentially more exciting corporate world.

The final member of the acquisition team, a man brought in specifically as acquisitions manager, was Dennis Amiss, MBE. A former Warwickshire and England cricketer, Amiss had enjoyed an enormously successful 25-year cricketing career and when he retired from cricket in 1987 there were plenty of companies anxious to use his fame, contacts and undoubted charm. Amiss had already met me on social occasions and when we met again at the end of 1987 I invited him to lunch and asked him if he would look after the acquisition side of the business. Amiss's initial reaction was favourable but his wife Jill was not in favour at all. I therefore invited Jill to the office and in a five-hour lunch lasting from one o'clock until six convinced her that working for a funeral director was not the end of the world. Indeed, working for the most dynamic funeral director in the country was actually going to be very exciting. They were convinced and Dennis joined on 1 February 1988 as director of acquisitions, research, and public relations. Within days he went to Buckingham Palace to receive his MBE.

However before Amiss joined, Hodgson had continued to acquire during 1987, buying W. H. Wigley in London for £415,000 in February and within days E. Seymour in St Albans for £325,000. The acquisitions since flotation had now cost Hodgson £2.4 million, and it was now able to exploit its position as a public company by issuing 1.76 million shares at 170p to raise £2.85 million net of expenses. Such was the image of the company's record that the stock-market took the issue of more paper in its stride, the *Investors Chronicle* commenting: 'Fair value even though the shares are much more highly rated than those of other undertakers.' The existing shares jumped 16p to 200p on the news. The real excitement, however, was yet to begin.

At various stages of a business career, whether buying or selling, you have to do 'the deal'. If you get it right, you have underpinned and correctly exploited all the hard work connected with the day-to-day running of the business; if you get it wrong, you could completely wreck all that hard work. Some deals are bigger and more important than others: the acquisition of Ingall's was an important deal for me.

On 2 April 1987 under the headline, 'Major deal on the cards at Hodgson Holdings', the *Birmingham Post* announced that I had asked the Stock Exchange to suspend dealings in Hodgson pending an announcement. In bear markets, suspensions usually imply disaster, but in bull markets they foretell glad tidings. As the *Post* correctly predicted: 'Watchers of the way Mr Hodgson has pursued his ambition to establish a national chain took the move as a signal that House of Fraser has accepted his offer for their considerable funeral operations.'

Ingall's originally was an engineering company, based in Wolverhampton, that had diversified into funerals. In 1985, Birmingham Co-op had made an offer for them, and, ironically, Ingall's, not keen to be part of the

Co-op, had considered making an offer for Hodgson's, still at that time a private company. However, once the Co-op made a formal offer it was not possible for Ingall's to make an offer for Hodgson. Following the Co-op's offer of 80p a share for Ingall's, the House of Fraser, which already had considerable funeral interests in Scotland through its ownership of Wylie and Lockhead, entered the battle and offered 110p. The Co-op did not react, and Ingall's became part of House of Fraser.

Over the next two years the House of Fraser underwent great traumas as Tiny Rowland and the Al Fayeds fought over ownership. The Al Fayeds ultimately were successful, but decided by early 1987 that some disposals were necessary. The funeral operations were not seen as a core business for the future, and it became known that House of Fraser was keen to sell Ingall's. I was naturally interested, but Ingall's was too big for me. It was conducting 22,000 funerals a year with a turnover of approximately £16 million and the asking price was £30 million; despite its rapid expansion, Hodgson was conducting only 9,500 funerals a year. I felt the market, if not the exchange itself, would not let me do it, but in talking to various contacts and advisers I was told by the man who had supported me before flotation, John Jay, that I must. It was an opportunity I must seize, a quantum leap I must make.

Well, I thought, perhaps there could be a way, if I only bought half. This may be acceptable, and half a cake is better than none. So I needed a partner. I turned to one of the other public companies, Kenyon Securities, and offered the managing director, Michael Kenyon, a deal whereby we would take half each. Kenyon turned me down. I then telephoned Bruce McDougall at the Co-operative Wholesale Society, the CWS, and asked, 'Do you want to make a deal?' McDougall replied, 'If I want to buy the House of Fraser Funeral Division I don't need Hodgson Holdings.' 'Naturally,' I said, 'you could offload the bits you don't want to other Co-op Societies and get some cash back. You certainly don't need me for that. However, I am going to buy the bloody thing and you'll get nothing. You may have the other societies behind you but I have the London Exchange behind me. Remember you telephoned me at the time of the flotation of Hodgson and said that you'd heard the capitalization was £7.2 million but that had to be a joke. Well the market cap., ten months later, is over £14 million and who's laughing now? I was willing to share the deal so that we didn't push the price any higher but if you don't want to talk. . . .' 'Okay, okay. Let's have lunch,' he replied.

Bullshit baffles brains so they say. That had been pure bullshit – but it had worked. Furthermore one thing was correct – I had made up my mind that I was going to buy 'the bloody thing'.

Hodgson and the Co-op were granted time by the House of Fraser to get their act together, and, having signed joint heads of agreement, the two were just about to make an offer when we were told that Ingall's had been sold for £30 million to another party. I was devastated. It was a Friday afternoon. I had to go to a dinner that evening. I sat there quite numb. A friend, who was a corporate finance adviser in the City said, 'Forget it. It's gone. It's lost.' 'Oh no it's not. I refuse to lose it,' I replied.

CCM, our corporate finance advisers, had given up, the Co-op had given up, but I found an ally in Tim Seymour of County NatWest, the Co-op's corporate advisers. We talked over the weekend, and that resulted in Tim telephoning Brian Walsh, the chief executive of the House of Fraser and telling him, 'You're not a gentleman.' Walsh, an Australian, hated the thought of that.

Walsh invited our respective teams to see him, and as a result we offered him £31 million to clinch the purchase. After checking with Al Fayed, Walsh agreed but insisted on a completion of the deal within three weeks to suit House of Fraser tax requirements. I was elated, but then received a body-blow from the takeover panel. It was such a big deal that they insisted that Hodgson Holdings could not pay more than £15.5 million without approval from its shareholders, which could not be done within the three-week deadline. As the agreed price was £31 million, Hodgson's share was just acceptable. But now the takeover panel decreed that Hodgson and CWS could not split the English and Scottish parts of the House of Fraser funeral division as they wished. One had to buy the English section, Ingall's (in order that a long-form accounting report could be prepared for the Hodgson Holdings stock holders) and the other the original Wylie and Lockhead, in Scotland. CWS said it was happy with Wylie and Lockhead, but this meant that Hodgson would have to pay £17.5 million because the English division was larger.

Here was an impossible dilemma. Try as Hodgson's brokers did to solve the problem with the panel, they could not succeed; nor could Price Waterhouse, our accountants, or Edge & Ellison, our solicitors, think of a solution.

I found the solution not because I was more intelligent, but because I wanted the deal more; I refused to lose it. I had realized that if the House of Fraser left the creditors in the deal, the price would be reduced by that amount, and on checking discovered we would only have to pay them £15.3 million, and therefore would be back under the limit. That was the major problem solved, but there were others, and three weeks was a very short time to complete a deal to everyone's satisfaction.

We had to grant many concessions early on in case the 'other' purchasers were invited back. However, as we approached the deadline, and the House of Fraser were stuck with us, we got those back and were able to end up with a satisfactory deal for our shareholders.

Just before the completion date, a massive tactical meeting between

Hodgson and the Co-op and their ever-growing armies of advisers took place at the Co-op International Bank in the City.

Tim Seymour shook our side by opening with a statement which said that the Co-op was not happy with its long-form report and wanted to negotiate the price down, postpone the deal and if they did not get what they wanted, call the whole thing off. (They suspected we were having problems with the panel and would instantly agree to this proposal.) I announced we were happy with our long-form report, and asked to be relesed from the heads of agreement with them in order to buy both Ingall's and Wylie and Lockhead.

My team looked horror-struck, but I was prepared to call their bluff as I had realized that if I bought Ingall's now, my market capitalization would rise and therefore could return for Wylie and Lockhead that autumn without having a problem with the panel. I also suspected the House of Fraser would agree, because half by the deadline with a promise to buy the other half within a few months was better than no deal at all before the tax deadline.

The Co-op asked for an adjournment. Within ten minutes they were back, they had changed their minds about their long-form report, and the deal was on again. I continued to refuse to lose it.

On completion day, a Saturday, all parties and their advisers gathered in the City. The day became the subject of a BBC Radio 4 programme. It found the protagonists arguing in a dozen rooms, making points here, conceding points there, removing jackets and loosening ties as the hours went by and physical and mental temperatures rose. What I was after was Ingall Industries, along with its debtors, creditors, and its ongoing state of play, for £15.3 million. What the Co-op had its sights on was Wylie and Lockhead, an operation valued at £13.5 million. What both Hodgson's and the Co-op were up against was the House of Fraser's insistence that if one side of the deal did not go through, neither would the other: it wanted a £28.8 million package, which had to be agreed by midnight.

Discussions had been going on for twelve hours when something unexpected cropped up concerning Ingall's articles of association. It was a point I could not concede on behalf of my shareholders, and I made this clear in the most dramatic way I could think of – by picking up my jacket and making for the door, pausing only to say, 'Good evening, gentlemen.' I knew that somebody would react pretty quickly, and it turned out to be Simon Renton of McKenna's, the House of Fraser solicitors. Brows were mopped and the talking re-started, but the atmosphere remained as edgy as ever.

Shortly before midnight, Brian Walsh, the House of Fraser chief executive, came in to sign the agreement – but agreement had still not been reached. In true cliff-hanger style, there were just two minutes to go. I led my team to the room where everyone else was waiting. Like a sheriff exploding into a saloon, I shoved open the doors and faced my audience. The five words I then spoke were the most important ones I had ever uttered on behalf of my firm: 'Gentlemen, we have a deal!'

It was a deal which brought Hodgson Holdings' value to £30 million and gave it responsibility for 23,000 funerals a year, 4% of all the funerals in England and Wales. We had overtaken Kenyon and Great Southern at a stroke, and were now the unrivalled major force in our profession. I had refused to lose it, and indeed had won it – but it did not actually become official until it had been signed, and it could not be signed until a signature representing each of the parties had been put alongside every change that had been made to every original document. The result was that the celebrations were well under way by the time the final signature had been written – but no one could have expected anything different, after 15 hours of tough, sometimes rough, talking.

McKenna's threw a dinner in celebration. It had come within two minutes of having to be thrown out of the window, but it was a good gesture, diminished only by the Co-op party's insistence that they were going home instead of enjoying the hospitality. They explained that it was so late – but then their departure was unexpectedly delayed because it took a remarkably long time for them to arrange transport, notwithstanding the number of Co-op funeral limousines in London.

At the age of thirty-seven I was now the force that mattered in my profession. I was on an unimaginable high, and I was in no hurry to come down.

The *Birmingham Post* was able to pat itself on the back for its prediction:

Just as we indicated when Hodgson Holdings' shares were suspended at the beginning of April, Mr Howard Hodgson, Handsworth's funeral director extraordinary, has clinched a deal to buy the former Ingall Industries business from House of Fraser – thereby increasing the size of his fast-growing business by 140 per cent.

To raise the money – and another 1.5 million for good measure – he is issuing new shares at 240p through a placing and open offer to existing shareholders at 240p, compared with a 275p suspension price, on the basis of five new shares for every eight held.

The institutions have been persuaded to go easy with their fees by the guarantee of more than 50 per cent of the new shares. This is possible since Mr Hodgson and Sumit, holder of 4 per cent of the equity, have agreed not to take up their entitlements. The effect will be to dilute Mr Hodgson's controlling stake to about 30 per cent.

The official document sent out to all shareholders inviting them to subscribe in an Open Offer for 7,083,000 new ordinary shares at 240p could hardly keep the euphoria out of its explanations for the reasons for the deal, which were stated as:

The policy of your Company is expansion through acquisition – a philosophy which to date has been put successfully into practice by the purchase of small and medium funeral businesses.

The formula used is simple but effective with three ingredients being critical to its success. Firstly, the business acquired is brought swiftly and efficiently into the Group structure by means of detailed check lists containing over 150 procedures and operating methods to be implemented. Secondly, economies of scale are made (without detriment to the high standard of service expected by the Board) as soon as practically possible. Finally, and in conjunction with the first two steps, rigorous and regular reporting requirements applied consistently throughout the Group are introduced. Your Board are confident that the formula can be applied successfully to this substantial operation – indeed in some ways its application is made easier in that staff and managers are used to working within the environment of a large organisation.

Since your Company came to the Unlisted Securities market in June 1986 it has followed an aggressive acquisition policy which (before taking into account Ingall's) has already changed the number of funerals arranged per annum from 5,600 to approximately 9,500 (an increase of almost 70 per cent). The acquisition of Ingall Industries should increase the total number of funerals arranged per annum to approximately 23,000 representing a market share of almost four per cent in England and Wales.

The acquisition of Ingall Industries will benefit Hodgsons in that overnight it will add 52 new outlets to the Company – both complementing current geographical operations of the Group and extending into areas not previously penetrated. Your Company now has a unique opportunity to apply its tried and tested formula to Ingall's so adding a new impetus to the Group's activities. The margins of Ingall's are below those achieved by Hodgsons. This is a position which your Directors are confident can be rectified swiftly to the advantage of shareholders.

The proposed acquisition, as is self-evident from the dramatic increase in the market share which Hodgsons will command, is a major and significant development for your Company. Your Board is confident it can meet the challenge.

The CWS side of the deal soon ran into trouble with the Monopolies and Mergers Commission as its purchase of House of Fraser's Scottish division gave it 21,000 of Scotland's 50,000 funerals leading the *Guardian* to announce under the ponderous headline: 'DEATH: IT'S NOT ALL AT THE CO-OP' that 'the CWS is already the country's largest undertaker but a recent move to expand its Scottish business is to come under scrutiny of the MMC'.

I pressed on with three more acquisitions already under negotiation at the time of the Ingall's deal. The first was Ashton Ebbutt, the same firm that I had escaped to when fired by my father in the early 1970s. At £2.2 million it was easily the biggest purchase so far – apart from Ingall's – and gave me twelve offices in the London area. At the same time I mopped up a small, loss-making Manchester undertaker, John G. Ashton, for £106,000, and Coyne's of Liverpool, conducting some 1,000 funerals a year, for £1 million.

The media had nothing but praise for the deals done in the short year since flotation. There were further references to Hanson though *Marketing* felt a better comparison was Gerald Ratner, who had also greatly expanded a family business by acquisition. The *New Statesman* was more adventurous:

> A Roman Polanski lookalike with long hair, cuff-links and buttoned-up, buttoned-down air, he talks smoothly of creating new market opportunities for his trade and planning a more comprehensive service for clients with financial advice for the bereaved.

While I was negotiating the deals with Ingall's, Ashton Ebbutt, and Coyne's of Liverpool, the country was moving towards a general election. The previous election had been in June 1983 and another was not necessary until June 1988, but governments do not like to feel hemmed in, and as the opinion polls remained favourable – inflation fell to nearly 3%, the stock-market was booming, and the economy growing – Margaret Thatcher called an election for June 1987.

If Mrs Thatcher's first term, from May 1979 until June 1983, had purged the country of its bad habits under the so-called consensus governments, both Tory and Labour, in the 1960s and 1970s, the second term, from June 1983 to June 1987, completed the purge and began to give the people some of the rewards they had voted for. Just as the Argentinian General Galtieri had provided a convenient whipping boy – 'the enemy without' – for the first administration, the miners' leader, Arthur Scargill – 'the enemy within' – stepped up as the adversary to be overcome in the second.

The miners had effectively scuppered Heath's Tory administration, first in 1972 and finally in 1974. Now there was to be another match, but this time the government had done some proper training. One of the reasons the miners had been successful in the 1970s was due to their organization of secondary picketing. They won a famous, though some see it as Pyrrhic, victory when they forced the police to close the vital Saltley Power Station to incoming lorries because of the danger to human life from the violence of mining pickets. This victory led the miners – and Scargill in particular as he had organized the pickets – to believe they would always win. They had the guts and determination to see a battle through, while the forces of law and order would show restraint.

They were wrong. First, the law on secondary picketing was changed and, second, Margaret Thatcher was capable of meeting the forces of 'wrong' with her forces of 'right', well-armed, and just as violent. She brought in a tough, American-trained, Scots businessman, Ian MacGregor, to give the coal board some backbone, and mobilized the police forces of the country – having been careful to give them substantial pay rises – to counter the miners. Finally, she waited until coal stocks were high. (She had backed away from a confrontation in 1981 when advised that stocks were not high enough.)

It was an epic battle. Mining communities generally are impervious to public opinion, especially as they feel that most of it comes from softies in the south who do not do a proper day's work anyway. They also have a huge loyalty to their union, the National Union of Mineworkers (NUM). Their leader, Arthur Scargill, was a charismatic, charming, and extremely eloquent figure who knew how to express their feelings for them. And he was right: the coal board was planning to close many pits and reduce the number of mineworkers substantially.

The miners, however, or more truthfully the NUM, made two errors of judgement. The NUM failed to hold a ballot to authorize strike action, which led to a significant minority, the Nottinghamshire miners, refusing to strike. This meant that coal stocks were being replenished sufficiently to avoid a repetition of Heath's three-day weeks. And they did not realize that Margaret Thatcher played to win, whatever the cost, and the cost in terms of both money and strain on social cohesion was high. Nevertheless, most felt it was a price worth paying: it was the final nail in the coffin of union supremacy over the government.

The strongest union in the country, the NUM surrendered unconditionally after a year. Allied to the union legislation, so skilfully handled through Parliament by Jim Prior and Norman Tebbitt, this victory restored the balance of power in industrial relations. Management had been given back the right to manage, and governments to govern. Most people were grateful and relieved, and Mrs Thatcher won another victory in 1987.

Mrs Thatcher also was aided, as was I, by the continuing bull market on the London Stock Exchange, and indeed throughout the world's stock-markets. The Conservative Government had set out to create more private shareholders, a sector that had been declining steadily since the War. The

Conservative Party eventually grasped privatization, or de-nationalization, to its bosom, although initially they were not so sure. But Mrs Thatcher was adamant about de-nationalization, saying in 1981: 'The two great problems of the British economy are the monopoly nationalized industries and the monopoly trade unions.'

In Nicholas Ridley she found the man to put flesh on the bones of her conviction. An old Etonian, he burned with a conviction for the free market. Hugo Young captures the spirit of Ridley's approach: 'Ridley believed that the nationalized industries were from every point of view deplorable. Over-subsidized, uncompetitive and monopolistic, they could not but be inefficient and under-productive...' Ridley believed the nationalized industries to be over-subsidized, inefficient and under-productive. They were monopolies that lacked incentive and competition. Ridley believed things must change. The nationalized industries should be set financial targets and forced to meet them even if it meant wholesale closure of large unprofitable plants. Managers must manage, free from government interference or shelter. Ridley sought to make the nationalized industries resemble public companies by the introduction of tough management, the reduction of union power and the necessity to hit targets. Privatization? No, that was too big a step, even for the right-wing Ridley in the autumn of 1978. The destruction of the nationalized industries was to happen amid much joy and little sorrow, even in Labour ranks, much later.

Ridley's plans found a ready response in Margaret Thatcher, but in her first term only a modest beginning was made in the onslaught on these state monoliths. Some British Rail assets were sold, British Gas lost some of its monopolies, British Telecom was exposed to some competition on its equipment supplies, but the only full privatizations were the National Freight Corporation, some of the docks, and the chemical and electronic firm, Amersham International. The second Thatcher Administration, however, was more confident, and to keep the momentum going, the sale of public assets made possible large cuts in direct taxation in the budgets of 1985 and 1986.

The whole process helped to sustain the bull market that had begun in 1982, and swung the necessary voters to keep the Conservatives in power when some of their traditional middle-class supporters were beginning to have doubts about what had become known as Thatcherism. An analysis of those who voted Conservative in 1987 shows how important the skilled manual worker turned out to be: the Tory share of the manual workers' vote, at 36%, was higher than in any election since the War; in 1979 Labour still secured 45% of the skilled worker vote, not much less than in 1974; by 1987 Thatcherism had eroded this to 34%. The opinion polls showed that these were the very people who were buying their own council houses and the shares of the freshly privatized British this and British that.

Many people who apparently know have stated that the three great reforming Prime Ministers of the 20th century were Lloyd George, Clement Attlee and Margaret Hilda Thatcher. One a Liberal, one a Socialist and one a Conservative. Moreover most of Thatcher's reforms were concerned with undoing the negative effects of Attlee's. The frontiers of the state were pushed back as nationalized industry after nationalized industry was privatized, their quoted shares often being bought by their trade union employees, causing a massive rise in the number of people in the country owning shares, especially those in the unions. Thatcher's capitalist democracy for all was beginning to take shape.

As Thatcherism and the bull market rolled on, Hodgson Holdings rolled with them. The personal and corporate publicity I received in abundance was of great benefit in keeping the Hodgson share price on the boil. As the *Director* reported in 1987 shortly after completion of the Ingall's deal:

> Just how he has fired the City's imagination can be judged by the comparative p/e ratios of the three publicly quoted funeral companies. Kenyon Securities languishes in the high teens; Great Southern Group, the Sussex based firm run by the Field family, sits in the low twenties; Hodgson is double that.

My seventeenth buy was a small firm in Bedford, R. Circet, handling 165 funerals a year, which I bought for £145,000 in August. Later the same month I added Tovey & Morris of Newport, Gwent, for £160,000, adding a further 125 funerals. Within a week came the nineteenth, Howard's of Stockport – a very small firm. Large acquisitions at this pace were becoming more difficult.

On 19 October 1987 the bull market bandwagon appeared to be derailed. The City and most of the stock-markets of the world were wallowing in an orgy of self-love; the Tories had won again and were in for another five years; serious money was there for the taking: the markets were on the up after the usual summer hiccup, when – BANG! It all *stopped*. First New York, then Tokyo and Hong Kong, then London, then New York again, then Hong Kong, Tokyo and Sydney, then London, Paris, and Frankfurt all turned into screaming, yelling pits of hysteria as the market lost a year's gains in twenty-four hours. It was only twelve years, or 3,000 trading days since the whole FT 30 Index had stood at 147 (the same year I bought my father's business). Now it lost 183.7 points in a single day. If that was dramatic, the Dow Jones fell by over 500 points, and it was only five years, or 1,250 trading days, since that index had been around 600.

If everyone over forty can remember what they were doing when they heard President Kennedy had been shot, every serious investor will remember 'Black Monday' in October 1987. It was called 'Black Monday' after the Wall Street 'Black Monday' in 1929, itself named after 'Black Friday', 24 September 1869, when a group of punters tried to corner the gold market, causing a panic, which led to a crash and a depression.

The markets steadied after a 25% fall, although that was 25% for respectable stocks. Some of the shooting stars were down 50, 60 or even 70%, and in any case were unsellable except in tiny quantities. Was the party over? Would companies like Hodgson, dependent for their growth on acquisitions, and dependent for their acquisitions on a strong and rising share price, be able to continue as before? It was bound to have an effect. The Hodgson takeover of Ingall's had been financed by a £17 million rights issue at 240p. Subsequently the shares had risen to 296p, but the Crash brought them back sharply to 200p.

The takeover train kept rolling. On 22 December 1987, just over two months after the Crash, the *Financial Times* announced:

> Hodgson Holdings, USM-quoted funeral director, has acquired four more funeral directors for a total of £800,000 cash, including 212,000 for properties. The purchases will add about 800 funerals a year making Hodgson's total more than 28,000.

The effect on the share price was the same as in earlier, headier days – it moved up a few pence to 208p – if a little more muted.

Nevertheless, the damage to the Hodgson share price was having an effect on my ambitions. I wanted to buy Wylie and Lockhead, the part of the House of Fraser in Scotland that the CWS had bought, but now had to sell under instructions from the Mergers and Monopolies Commission. I was constrained to ask my shareholders for more money in another rights issue with the price below the 240p they had stumped up for the Ingall's purchase.

The bandwagon had been halted but, in hindsight, the tight schedule for the acquisition of Ingall's in spring 1987 was a blessing, as the deal might never have been done at all after the Crash, and if it had, it would have been much less attractive with our share price down at 200p.

DOS AND DON'TS IN DEAL-MAKING

Although these mainly apply to the acquisition deal, most apply to any deal, which means dealings with other organizations, whether you are buying or selling in the negotiation of contracts.

● Think through the aim of the deal clearly. Then think through the probable outcome if you are successful.

- Plan the financing. Produce a business plan and examine how much capital will have to be raised, from which source, at what cost, and for what return.

- Plan a strategy for the deal with your team, including who is responsible for what and who talks to whom on the other side. Keep yourself in reserve as much as possible. This will give you greater flexibility to change direction without appearing to do U-turns.

- Open with a sensibly low price. Do not open too high in case you are forced higher and either pay too much or lose the deal. Do not open too low because an insult to the proposed vendor at this stage could lose you the deal.

- Try and work out whether your competitors are interested in the same deal, and if so what they could afford to pay.

- Know how important any deal is in relation to other prospective deals you wish to do.

- Never, never pay too much for a deal, especially if it is a very large acquisition and involves a great amount of gearing. If interest rates rise and the cost of the gearing exceeds the profits generated, then you could be seriously jeopardizing the whole business.

- Never sound too keen, and never give the impression that the target is the only fish in the sea. If the other side thinks they have got you, then they will concentrate on whether they want to do the deal, and if they do, how much extra they can get. If they believe you may be looking elsewhere, they will try and make the deal more attractive to you.

- Always tell the vendor you will call *him*. So that you can call at your psychological advantage, rather than the other way round.

- Be flexible enough to change your strategy, but always calculate the effect of any change.

- Keep talking the strategy through with your team.

- Always have at least two people at meetings – one talking and the other observing. The observer can gain much insight into the other camp's thoughts, and who is playing which rôle on their side. Understanding the other side is very important and often the key to doing a good deal.

• Never take a phone call directly from the other side unless you know exactly what you are going to say. A sudden, unrehearsed answer could cost you a lot of money, or even the deal.

• Be aware of timing. Use it to your advantage if possible. Try to avoid getting boxed in. If this happens, the pressure is on you, and the other side has a clear advantage.

• If you plan to do many deals and acquire a good reputation, remember that a good deal is a fair deal. You can be hard, but do not be dishonest.

CHAPTER 6

GOING PUBLIC

Y ou must want to 'go public' for the right reasons. You must go to the stock-market because it is right for your company and the company's future growth. In this way you and your stockholders have the same goals.

In the 1980s too many companies went to the USM for the wrong reasons, that is, just to get old money out (sell a portion of the existing ordinary shares). Some people saw the USM as a vehicle whereby they could sell part of their company to public institutions and become personally rich while still owning the majority of the stock and controlling their business. They believed they could have their cake and eat it. Such companies usually had unhappy experiences, both for the investing institutions and for the selfish family management: the institutions were disappointed by the company's future performance, and the management, having had no past experience of being held accountable, resented having to explain their lack of growth to impatient stockholders.

There are many misconceptions about institutional stockholders. Private businessmen who lack confidence and hide behind autocratic behaviour often fear that institutions could be on the phone all the time demanding meetings to talk about the company, or ganging up to remove the chief executive and his co-directors. All of this is nonsense. In the case of most USM flotations, the controlling family remains the largest shareholder. However, even if they could, the institutions have no intention of removing the chief executive or directors, other than in extraordinary circumstances. As long as the institutions are properly informed by way of the accounts and institutional meetings, which are necessary at the time of placings, rights issues, preference issues, and so on, they will be happy to be seen perhaps once a year.

Well-informed stockholders are much more likely to be loyal, and therefore buyers rather than sellers of your stock. You obviously want more buyers than sellers because you want the price to rise, not only because this affects your personal wealth, but because the higher the price of your stock the greater the market capitalization, the greater the flexibility you have to use that paper to expand your business yet further – which is exactly why you came to the market. A good investor relations or public relations company, if used correctly, can be invaluable in keeping your stockholders informed.

PLAYING THE GAME

You are now coming into a new arena, and you must learn to play this game quickly and correctly. You can be a little bit of an *enfant terrible*, but not too much; you can cock your hat at its rules, but do not try to change them and never make statements or forecasts that cannot be substantiated or met as the City has a very long memory.

Respect the City for what it is good at, but do not be overawed. You know more about your business than anyone else. You were its creator and the chief architect that led it to where it is today.

At the time of Hodgson Holdings flotation I had to make my first institutional presentation to approximately fifty or sixty institutional salesmen from the company that was floating us. It involved a slide show – but the slides did not arrive. Twenty minutes past. My sponsoring broker said, 'This is going to be a disaster.' I said, 'I am not associated with disasters', but I became shy and nervous. The slides did eventually arrive, but then had to be put in the machine. I was going for my fourteenth pee in about twenty-five minutes when an institutional salesman who was waiting in the corridor caught my elbow. 'Don't be nervous,' he said. 'Always remember, you built this company, you brought it here today. What have they ever done? You get in there and tell them the way it is.' Which is precisely what I did.

FLOTATION

You have decided you want to float your company, and have found that the institutions would be prepared to invest in the same. You are attracted to the City, and the City is apparently attracted to you. We now have to arrange it so they can trade in your shares. This is called flotation.

THE TEAM

You need first to assemble the team that will work closely with you to achieve flotation. Normally this would include:

a firm of brokers (your corporate finance advisers and sponsors – you could use a merchant bank as your sponsors; however if you do you would still need brokers. Therefore unless a merchant bank has got you this far, and if they have they should certainly be your sponsors and will select good brokers for you, go straight to the brokers as you will skip a large fee);

accountants (the City prefers recognized names and therefore your existing accountants may have to resign);

solicitors (keep your current solicitor unless he or she is not up to the task, in which case, look at a large provincial partnership with experience in the field. Avoid large London solicitors as their fees are far too high, due much more to the location of their offices rather than the quality of their advice);

solicitors to the brokers, who will guide all parties through the necessary documentation. They will probably be a London firm, expensive, and you will have to pick up their fee. They will be a useful member of the team, but their loyalty is to the broker and not to you; this is especially true when you come to sign the placing agreement;

financial PR consultants are not to be confused with commercial public relations companies. You may have already been using a commercial public relations company during the years of growth in your company. Along with your brokers, financial PR consultants will ensure that institutions, analysts, and financial journalists are aware of your company's flotation and its future prospects. This will be achieved by organizing a series of meetings with institutional buyers and analysts, arranging for at least one private lunch with a journalist prior to flotation, and organizing a press conference at the time of flotation;

lastly, just on the periphery of the team, will be the **printers**, who will print that most important document called the prospectus. London brokers will tell you you need London printers. This is not necessarily true – provincial printers can match the quality and speed of operation, often at a fraction of the price.

So now you have assembled your team. Before you sit down together, ensure you have extracted watertight and satisfactory quotations from all external members. In each case the amount should be fixed, and it should be understood that this amount will not go up in the event of more work being carried out, or reduced in the event of less. By doing this, you are from day one in control of the cost of flotation. Do not be frightened to shop around if you are not pleased with the quotes you are given.

Assuming your company is a fairly small one being floated on the USM, with a proposed market capitalization of less than £10 million, here is an indication of the approximate fees you would have paid in 1992;

- **Brokers £60K.**

- **Accountants £30K.** Dependent on the extent of the work concerned with the long-form report, an accountant's report without which the flotation would not be achievable. Prior to flotation, if you were to use a venture capitalist, a long-form report would also be necessary. If you know at that time you are going to float the business, then it is possible to do a two-for-the-price-of-one deal. Indeed I did exactly that with Price Waterhouse when engaging the venture capital SUMIT prior to the flotation on the USM.

- **Solicitors £20K.** Again, dependent on the work undertaken, if this is to be done by your solicitors rather than the solicitors to the brokers, that is, the organization of all previous legal documents in the company, the verification notes concerning the prospectus, and so on, then your solicitor's fee will be higher and the solicitors to the brokers fee lower, and vice-versa.

- **Solicitors to the broker £15K.** See above.

- **Financial PR.** It is possible to achieve this for disbursement cost only on the basis that you will sign up the company on an annual retainer, which thereafter would be between £15,000-£25,000 per annum. It is important that you have confidence in these people because not only are they working for you at this moment, but you are going to have an ongoing relationship with them. Financial PR is not just about getting articles in the *Financial Times*. It is about keeping institutions informed so they will want to continue with their holding, or even increase it, and potential new investors who by being made aware of the company will wish to buy into the stock.

- **Printers £20K.** This depends very much on the quality of the prospectus and the number you are having printed. The fee can be considerably reduced by not having too many printed proofs, especially early on when typed, photocopied manuscripts are adequate; and by negotiating a high percentage of author's corrections without extra charges being made. Closely scrutinize the amount charged for author's corrections in the event they become applicable.

The professionals will put you under pressure concerning the cost of flotation. They will tell you that such amounts do not go through your profit-and-loss account, and therefore affect the company's performance. You must remember, however, on behalf of all stockholders, that the amounts paid out come from the tax-paid cash reserves of the company, which belong to the stockholders and are therefore not to be wasted.

DRAFTING

Next, your brokers will call a meeting of the team, and issue a timetable and responsibility programme, which tells you who does what and when between now and the date of flotation. It is most important you run through this and understand the terminology and responsibilities – and not just where they apply to you and your fellow directors but to each and every one of the team members. You must have a complete picture in your mind of what is going to happen in the next two months. Do not be frightened to question anything you are not sure about; do not be embarrassed about your ignorance. Remember that the only reason anyone is there is because you are floating your company, and you are paying them.

The meeting will then turn to the ghastly pastime called 'drafting'. Someone, probably a director from the firm of brokers, will have had a go at writing a prospectus. It will probably be technically inaccurate, but the exercise has to start somewhere. Over the next few weeks, the prospectus, which tells the potential investor about the company, its history, its future prospects, corporate policy, accounts, and so on, will take shape.

Try not to have too many people involved in drafting or the whole process will become incredibly laborious and slow, with the accountants commenting on the English, solicitors on the technical aspect, and the brokers on the position concerning the law – yes, everyone starts interfering in everyone else's business. Grown men can sit round a table late at night, discussing whether in a particular sentence there should be a colon or semi-colon for over 45 minutes – incredible.

Moreover, it always amused me that the fifth draft seemed to be the same as the third. Everyone had felt the third was good then a week later sat down and after much deliberation improved it to the fourth. The following week the fourth was further improved by writing the fifth – but wait a minute the fifth is now like the third.

I so hated drafting that, having religiously attended every drafting meeting at the time of the flotation of Hodgson Holdings, in 1986 I refused to go to any of the ones following. I told them, 'You guys write it, and if I like it I will sign it.' I would then appoint one lawyer and Hodgson Holdings Company Secretary to draft the whole document. They did this more quickly, more efficiently, and at much less expense.

At the end, you have a prospectus. Because this document has had a lot of time, attention, love, and care lavished on it, it is sensible to spend a little extra on a good presentation. Ensure that you are happy with the typesetting of the new company name (plc). If you are going to have the corporate logo altered or touched-up, now is the time to do it. Ensure that the prospectus has a fine cover, is printed in corporate colours, and is as lively and readable as possible. You have put a lot of work into building this company and bringing it to the market. At the final moment, do not 'spoil the ship for half-penny's worth of tar'.

Readers of this book who remember the Hodgson Holdings prospectus may comment – 'Mais quel hypocrite' due to the fact that there were no photographs in the Hodgson Holdings prospectus. This was not my doing. The Stock Exchange panel decided that it would not be terribly tasteful to have funereal photographs in Hodgson Holdings prospectus. At the time I thought this to be laughable as they had just allowed a ladies lingerie firm to display page three type photos throughout its prospectus.

Next we must turn out attention to the verification notes, which are a series of questions and answers: the questions being written by the solicitors to the brokers, you supplying the answers, thus verifying that the facts in the prospectus are correct. All of this can be extremely tedious, but it is something that is essential, as the Stock Exchange wishes companies to float with prospectuses that are accurate and truthful in every detail and comply with the law of the land.

One of the questions that I was asked in the verification notes was – verify in the late 1950s and early 1960s that the number of funerals conducted by Hodgson & Sons Ltd fell due to demolition of property. I replied 'no houses equals no people – no people equals no deaths – no deaths equals no funerals – fucking QED.'

THE PLACING AGREEMENT

Then there is the placing agreement, a legal document made between the broking house (your sponsor for the flotation) and your company. Ensure that your solicitors fight hard over the indemnity terms that are placed upon you and your fellow directors, especially those concerning non-executive directors. While it is highly unlikely that such indemnities will be called upon, it has always seemed to me quite unfair that a part-time non-executive director on only £5,000 per annum should sign such indemnities.

SHARE PRICING

It is at about this time that you and the brokers should sit down to do something of great importance to you – the current shareholders – and the institutions – your future partners – that is, agreeing finally and firmly the offer share price.

Setting the price is not only influenced by your company's performance, but the market's view of your industry, and the current state of the market in general. Naturally, you will want it to be high because you are selling some of the company; the brokers will want it to be lower because they have to place the stock with their institutional clients. On their side, the institutional salesmen will want to get the best deal for their clients, the institutions, but you will have support from their corporate finance team, whose client is you.

No doubt you will be angry if the company places at 110p and the price doubles on the first morning, which means the shares were placed too cheaply. This would hardly be a recommendation for the corporate finance team, and therefore they will try to strike the right balance. If the shares move to a premium (remember a discount is in nobody's interest – certainly not yours), of say 5–20% then the price setting has been successful and all parties can feel pleased. The best market is an orderly market.

Over the two- to three-month period that all of this is happening, you and your finance director are devoting massive amounts of time to the flotation that normally would have been spent upon running your business. Ensure that your deputy chief executive, or whoever you have appointed to run the show while you are involved in the flotation, is completely looking after the day-to-day running, as if you are on holiday.

Try to avoid floating on the back of a forecast. If you have had three years' excellent growth, and can command the p/e ratio that gives you the share price you want, seriously consider doing this rather than going on the back of unpublished results some six months away. Obviously, if the inclusion of these future figures makes a massive difference to the capitalization of the company – which they may well, especially if you have been expanding considerably in the year of flotation – then go the forecast route. If the difference is not so acute, then do not, as there is an element of risk. If you do float on the strength of forecasted profits, ensure that it is a forecast that you will be able to achieve; failure to meet such a forecast could ruin your company's reputation in the City for several years to come.

PUBLIC RELATIONS

Next comes the press release. Obviously the public relations company and your brokers will have a considerable input concerning this. Remember, however, that you know the business better than anyone else and why you have floated it: only approve the press release when you are completely satisfied. As you approach the big day, ensure that your public relations company runs through the press conference presentation – not only what is said but who says it – and fires some potential questions at you so you know what to expect from the journalists. It is no good having a marvellous presentation if everyone becomes tongue-tied at the whiff of the first difficult question. If you know your subject and you speak confidently, you will account for yourself well.

Do not forget that once the tremendous excitement of the flotation is out of the way, it is essential that the institutional sales department of your brokers gives you good support in looking after the share price.

SHARE PRICE

The City is by and large short-sighted and far too concerned with short-term earnings-per-share (EPS), but it does know a good deal when it sees one. When many people in 1987 thought I had paid the Fayeds too much for the House of Fraser Funeral Divisions, the City understood that I had not. It understood that I had utilized the high value of my paper to make a deal that subsequently put earnings-per-share up from 6.6p to 11.6p within one year, almost doubling them. While so-called funeral 'experts' were busy appearing on the BBC 'Money Programme' to say that the price was too high, the City enthusiastically supported the deal, and they were proved to be right.

When you first bring a company to the market, you will be anxious about the share price, reaching for the *Financial Times* each morning to see what it is. If the price goes down you will complain bitterly to your brokers that people do not understand as if potential investors and brokers were really quite stupid and had not understood you on the first occasion. *Relax.* In the end, the City always gets your share price right; but be warned, because they will also get it right if it is too high.

The City is probably a better place since the October 1987 Crash. In 1987 it was fat, lazy, and charged far too much money (corporate finance-wise) for what it did. The institutional buyers seemed to be one position up from tea boy, and consisted of young men who were paid a great deal of money for knowing little or nothing about what their job entailed. By comparison, the Scottish career-minded institutional buying ladies were very good, and one had better know one's business before going to see them. However, following the 1987 Crash, and the low levels of institutional business since then, many of these *chubby young men* have got leaner, fitter, and have survived or left the City.

Traditionally, after the press conference there is the completion lunch when the directors, their wives, and the people involved in the flotation – the team – join together in celebration at lunch. It is a great day because it is a great achievement. For me it was a little sad because it was the end of three months that had been extremely exciting; I had loved every minute of it. Sit back, relax, and puff on your cigar. You have earned it. You have come a long way from the start of this book. You are now a millionaire, perhaps famous, and certainly the chairman of a public company – well done! But life has only just started – now you simply have a much better vehicle with which to race and win.

Left My mother described me as a pleasant and placid little boy. She later thought this to be laughably inaccurate.

Below The old Hockley office that I remember as a little boy. Families often queued up to make funeral arrangements during the annual flu epidemic.

Bottom The old man and me. He was so good looking and kind. The complete hero. I think I looked to a McCartney/Botham combination to replace him.

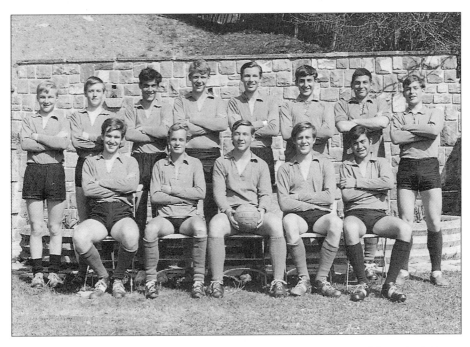

Above The 1964 Aiglon 1st XI Soccer. That's me back row second from the left; three years younger than the rest and it shows.

Below right It's 1975 and I now own Hodgson. The topper and tails may be nineteenth century, but the shirt and tie are horribly '70s.

Below The 1972 'report room' in N.W.M. Altrincham. John Firth (right) and I could spend 20 hours a day in there sometimes.

Above 1979 and the dedication of the Oaklands Funeral Home. Montefiore was sweet when in front of the camera and a pain when not.

Below 1982. A Sikh leader's funeral. I led 10,000 people on a six mile walk to the crematorium. It is only weeks after my son Charles' death.

Above 1986. Graham Hodson (second left), John Taylor and I pose with members of the ANZ Corporate Finance team outside the Stock Exchange.

Below Flotation. Once inside and on the floor of the exchange we know we have done it and it shows on all our faces.

Above 1986. *Business* magazine's 'Top 40 Under 40' award ceremony.

Right 1987. The press conference to announce the acquisition of Ingalls from the House of Fraser.

Below 1987. Barry Lewis' photograph in the *Sunday Times* magazine gets me noticed.

Above 1989. The Savoy launch of 'Dignity in Destiny'. David Meakin (second right) was Dignity's C.E.O. at the time. Today he runs Hodgson Securities.

Below 1988. I am presented to Her Majesty the Queen at St James's Palace.

Above 1990. Sir Harry Secombe and I launch the P.H.K.I. Bereavement Support programme in London.

Below 1991. Hodgson & Partners Ltd is launched at the Berkeley Hotel in London. My ambition to work with John Gunn is fulfilled.

Above 1981. Our unique
and much loved son
Charles. He is never far
from my mind.

Left 1988. A photograph
taken for Maxwell's *Daily
Record* on the main lawns
of 'Edenwood'.

Below 1991. Davina smiles
at her adoring mother.
The boys and I call her
'Dinky'.

CHAPTER 7

INNOVATION

Some people in the City and in politics foresaw the end of the world in the Crash. Out in the real world, life continued much as before, and I was determined to continue my expansion and increase our market share by acquiring more independent funeral companies. I was locked in negotiations in late 1987 with the large London firm of Dottridge & Sons. Much to my chagrin I lost this, if temporarily, to my rival, Kenyon Securities, but Hodgson continued throughout 1988 to acquire further businesses. At the same time it was working on two new ancillary services: pre-arrangement and financial advice.

Welcomed with such headlines as: 'Pay first – and die later' (the *Financial Times*); 'The Bottom Line . . . and how to go in style' (*Today*); and 'Mr Death undertakes a revolution' (the *Sun*), Hodgson launched its 'Dignity in Destiny' programme in February 1989. The *Financial Times* greeted it as 'long-awaited', and indeed it had been a long time in gestation.

I had been talking about the concept of 'pre-arrangement' for several years, and in a totally unco-ordinated way my firm had been operating such a system, as clients came into our offices and expressed a desire to organize and pay for their funerals before they died.

There are other types of funeral packages on the market that were, and are confused with pre-arrangement. For many years life insurance companies have sold a term insurance policy that was supposed to pay funeral costs on the death of the insurer. These often were highly unsatisfactory in that they were not linked to the funeral, or the cost of it, in any way so that the payment by the insurance company did not necessarily cover the cost of the funeral and certainly did not take care of the funeral arrangements. Then there was 'pre-selection', whereby a client would decide what type of funeral, coffin, and flowers they wished, but would not pay anything towards the cost at that stage. Finally, there was 'pre-need,' whereby a large company such as ICI might give its employees the perk of paying for the funeral if they died prior to retirement, and, in the case of overseas employees, the repatriation expenses.

Throughout the second half of the 1980s, all four major funeral groups in the UK – the Co-op, Kenyon, Great Southern, and Hodgson – were launching pre-arrangement packages. The main competitor to the Hodgson plan was Great Southern's programme, 'Chosen Heritage', which had been launched in 1986 but had progressed slowly until it linked up with the charity Age Concern, which began to distribute details through its local support groups. By February 1989 'Chosen Heritage' claimed 7,500 subscribers and a monthly addition of 700. Southern offered two plans: a 'Simplicity Plan' costing £570 if paid in monthly instalments, or £525 if paid for in a single payment; and a 'Traditional Plan', which cost £765 monthly or £715 with a single payment. Our three 'Dignity' plans offered a similar choice and range of services: a guaranteed price for the choice of funeral; a guarantee on quality of service; payment by lump sum of monthly instalments; free advice by trained counsellors or affiliated funeral directors; the right to join at any age without medical examination; a separate trust fund with Lloyds Bank as custodian to provide security for the future cost of the funerals; and the backing of the largest publicly quoted funeral director in the country, as well as the worldwide charitable organization, Help the Aged.

'Dignity in Destiny' was launched with the announcement that B&C Ventures, part of the financial conglomerate British and Commonwealth Holdings, was taking a stake of 20% in the separate company, Dignity in Destiny Limited (Help the Aged was taking 5%, and Hodgson Holdings the remaining 75%). B&C Ventures was also providing Hodgson with £14.5 million capital by subscribing for 15 million 8.5p convertible preference shares at 100 per share.

British and Commonwealth originally had been a shipping company built up by the Cayzer family. After the Second World War it began to diversify into other fields, particularly aircraft operations. Its most notable and successful investment was a stake in and eventual acquisition of Bristow Helicopters. By the mid–1980s the Cayzer family had put their faith in the cool-headed men of the money markets. Having sold their last ship, they dropped 'Shipping' from the company name, and appointed as chief executive John Gunn, who had made his name building a money-broking operation based mainly in Hong Kong called Exco. Exco had been absorbed by B&C, and eventually the Cayzer family were bought out almost completely for a sum approaching £500 million. At the height of the bull market in the middle of 1987, B&C Holdings was one of the stars of the City, with its share price at an all-time high and John Gunn revered on all sides as one of the new Thatcherite financial tigers, a reputation that was fully justified.

The Crash of October 1987, following the initial, and in retrospect mistaken, reduction in interest rates, made life tougher for financial conglomerates such as B&C. Unfortunately they compounded their problems, first by choosing the wrong person to sell one of their money-broking subsidiaries to (he backed out of the deal), and, more significantly, by buying a computer-leasing company and paying over £400 million for it. Few queried the wisdom of this purchase at the time as Atlantic Computers was seen as one of the great success stories of an enterprise-encouraging government.

By late 1988 B&C were finding life tough on all fronts, but there was still a good deal of respect for John Gunn, as there is for this intelligent and sincere man today and the company remained a big player in the world of finance. He was to prove a welcome friend to me and I remain grateful to this day, for by late 1988 the truth is that Hodgson itself was in a slightly tricky position.

All of the publicly quoted funeral directors were generating growth by acquiring smaller funeral companies and by improving their performances through rationalization and centralization. Before my flotation in 1986 I had financed through borrowings, and in the year after flotation by the issuing of shares, twice in April 1987 and again in June 1987. This avenue was cut off by the market conditions following the 1987 Crash when shares fell generally by 25%, and the more volatile by much more.

Following the first Crash, everyone waited for a secondary Crash. In the Wall Street Crash of 1929 the market had recovered one-third of its fall in the early months of 1930, only to fall back in April and go on falling for another two years. This was the classic 'dead-cat-bounce' – even a cat will bounce if dropped from a great height before falling back, dead – and many expected it to happen again in April 1988. As a result, many investors, especially the private punters of the recent bull market, were frightened away. The market drifted on low volume – impossible conditions in which to raise money through a rights issue.

Nevertheless, I continued to acquire businesses, locked into a race with Kenyon and Great Southern to acquire the best of the available independents. By autumn 1988 Hodgson's borrowings were approaching £15 million and with interest rates rising sharply – after taking them down until the spring of 1988, the classic and in my opinion misguided response to a crisis of liquidity such as the October Crash, Chancellor of the Exchequer Nigel Lawson responded belatedly to the overheated economy by raising them sharply through the summer and autumn of 1988 – we needed an equity injection to ease the strains on our balance sheet.

I had been aware of the problem for months, and had been negotiating with the largest funeral company in the United States, Service Corporation International (SCI). While SCI had wanted to expand overseas and was keen to buy Hodgson, I had resisted but wanted to keep a dialogue going. I looked closely at SCI's request for me to market their 'Guardian' plan, which was basically an insurance plan. I did not like it, and did not feel it was the right vehicle with which to compete against Great Southern's 'Chosen Heritage'. I felt that 'Dignity in Destiny' was the correct plan for this country, and offered SCI a 50% stake in it, plus 20% of Hodgson Holdings for £15 million. After a big presentation to the SCI board in Houston, a deal was finally struck.

Everything was set up for the launch of 'Dignity in Destiny' – and an easing of the strain on Hodgson's balance sheet – when disaster struck. I was on my way to a reunion of the 'Top 40 Under 40' when I received a telephone call from Graham Hodson, who told me that he had just received a call from the finance director of SCI, who sounded unhappy. Hodson thought I should give him a call. I phoned from my car phone in London to Houston and got hold of SCI's finance director. He said their stock price had fallen $2 and they needed the money to buy in their own stock. The deal was off. Just like that, after six months of negotiation and an agreement – the deal was off!

I scarcely remember how I got through the reunion. There I was, with all these entrepreneurs, supposedly showing the media how successful we all still were, and a crucial deal had just fallen through. I needed to find £15 million in seven weeks. It was a bear market and most people thought I could not do it.

Then I had an inspiration. What about B&C? As it happened Dennis Amiss had played golf with John Gunn earlier in the summer at a Pro-Am tournament (ironically I had complained at the time – 'How many funeral directors are going to meet at this golf tournament, you're supposed to be the acquisitions director?'). I met Gunn and we talked mainly about cricket and now I wanted to talk to him about money. UBS Phillips and Drew (who had by now replaced CCM) were against it – division three, scraping the bottom of the barrel, not a good company, etc. In spite of this opposition I called John Gunn and we met. I explained what I wanted, and Gunn put his accountants to work thrashing out a deal. The B&C team and the Hodgson team struggled to reach agreement; Gunn was determined a deal should be struck, and in the end it was. It was criticized by at least one institution that had been approached by me earlier, which commented that the rate of interest, at 8.5%, was too high. I was furious and upbraided them at 'question time' during an institutional shareholders briefing saying: 'Interest rates generally are higher. It only has a three year, not an eleven year window like the quoted preference shares and its issue prevented a deeply discounted rights issue which would have sent Hodgson shares plunging. Furthermore, coming from you [it was the Prudential] it's a cheek as you turned it down because the coupon was not good enough but now for Mr Gunn it is too good!' The ever tactful Chris Marsh of UBS suggested we break for lunch.

In the document to shareholders offering them the chance to subscribe for up to 7,500,000 of 15,000,000 convertible preference shares it was clear why the money-raising exercise was necessary. It was not for the launch of 'Dignity in Destiny', though that would cost some more, it was to redress the Hodgson balance sheet following another huge acquisition programme. Sixty-four businesses had been acquired in the twelve months to 31 October 1988 at a cost of £26 million. I had not allowed the Crash of 1987 to slow me down, rightly or wrongly. Further acquisitions had been made since the end of the financial year as well.

The strategy of the board was laid out and bears reproducing here as it gives a snapshot of the company's position and its long-term aims:

The Group has achieved a rapid but carefully planned expansion, leading to the establishment of Hodgson Holdings as the largest and geographically best-represented publicly quoted national chain of funeral directors conducting in excess of 40,000 funerals on an annualised basis from more than 240 branches.

The strategy of the Group will continue to evolve and will include the following:

(i) the consolidation and rationalization of acquired businesses to increase the Group's core profitability;

(ii) the introduction of ancillary services, such as floral and monumental work to enhance turnover without the requirement for significantly increased capital resources;

(iii) the creation of a national corporate image which, while preserving the local identity of business acquired, portrays the Group's professional, secure, and up-to-date approach; and

(iv) the generation of further growth in market share through the introduction of pre-arranged funeral plans, and by the maximization of the business opportunities presented by the Group's substantial client base. An example of this is the recently announced association with Colonial Mutual Life Assurance Society Limited under which the Company will if requested introduce Colonial Mutual to clients of the Company for financial advice.

The tie-up with a life insurance company such as Colonial Mutual had been in my plans for a long time. Aware both of the need for my company to seek growth through selling ancillary services, and of relatives' need for professional financial advice at the time of a bereavement, I had seen the possibility of Hodgson offering financial services to its clients. However, it was a tricky area: I did not want to be accused of a hard sell to people who were emotionally disturbed. Furthermore, after some big insurance swindles in the 1960s and 1970s, the insurance industry was heavily circumscribed with rules and regulations.

In terms of selling 'Dignity in Destiny', the plan according to the offer document was to 'employ its own sales force to market its products on a commission basis'. The products also were to be sold by Help the Aged, and it was hoped that other professionals, principally solicitors and independent affiliated funeral directors, would also be involved in marketing.

As well as being a 5% shareholder in 'Dignity in Destiny', Help the Aged would receive 50p for every piece of business introduced. (Age Concern provided more than 50% of the plans written by 'Chosen Heritage'.)

The company was confident 'Dignity in Destiny' would provide: a further opportunity for growth through the securing of a future market share for Hodgson, as well as the generation of income in its own right; the further enhancement of the public profile of Hodgson Holdings, both through association with Help the Aged and the nationwide marketing of the 'Dignity in Destiny' name; and the extension of geographical representation through the affiliation of local funeral directors, who when they became vendors would probably follow us also.

As a result the press was fairly muted in its reception of 'Dignity', although it may have been confused by the simultaneous announcement of the link with Colonial Mutual, and also the announcement that Hodgson was to reduce further its gearing by valuing the brand names of the many companies it had bought. The *Financial Times* was noncommittal, confining itself to reporting the fact that 'a funeral director has become the first UK company to value the names of its subsidiaries in its accounts,' and that others – WPP Group, the advertising and marketing services company, among them – were considering doing the same. The *FT* did add, however, that:

> Hodgson Holding's decision to put a value of £42 million on the names of 80 groups of funeral companies could open a new chapter in the continuing debate over brand names. Last year, Ranks Hovis McDougall, the bakeries and food group, stirred up controversy in the accounting profession by becoming the first company to put a value on existing brands in its balance sheet. Hodgson argues that when buying a funeral business, goodwill and the value of the trade name are one and the same. The group says this is because undertakers rely on the loyalty of clients to that local name, generation after generation.

The *FT* also noted that Price Waterhouse, Hodgson's accountant, approved the change in accounting policy.

Tempus in *The Times* did not like it one bit:

> Mr Hodgson is unhappy about the effect of writing off goodwill against reserves, which all but wiped out shareholders' funds in the previous financial year. Under his new scheme funds are shown at £47.6 million.

> Any predator looking at his group would be likely to base its worth on the number of funerals conducted, he claims. With Hodgson now paying the equivalent of £1,500 a funeral for its latest acquisitions, this would value his group at about £75 million allowing for the work he has done in rationalizing his network.

> Hodgson's market capitalization is about half this: Mr Hodgson claims the company is something of a victim of its own success. The large number of acquisitions he has made is acting as a brake on further expansion.

The company dropped the plan later in the year, following its merger with Kenyon, and involvement with the French company Pompes Funèbres Générales (PFG). International ambitions made the valuing of trade names tricky.

As for 'Dignity in Destiny', it had a turnover of £400,000 in its first year, £1.5 million, in its second, and is on target for £5 million in its third. It has become a household name, and is fulfilling all its objectives.

It would have been easy to give up when some of the press and most of the funeral directing profession rounded on it. We did not because we knew we were right. We knew it was a good product; we knew there would be a market for it; we knew journalists have a poor record of being kind to pioneers; we knew the real reason the rest of the funeral profession did not like it was because they were frightened of it (in the past our market share advances had been by acquisition, now they might be by the 'Dignity' route, and therefore we might take market without having to buy it).

We had researched the market well; we knew the product backwards. Good enough? Hardly! We had not researched how to market the product. We had *assumed* (very dangerous – never make assumptions when concerned with business) that the marketing would work well by advertising for retired part-time staff who would be trained to sell the product by referral. It took us some time to work out that the way to market the product was to sell if off the page, backed by a computer database marketing system, with the client being sent the product directly and a counsellor visiting the client in their home to complete the paperwork. The discovery of the correct marketing technique signalled the take-off of the product. You must not only know the market and the product, but how to bring one to the other – the marketing route.

While I was negotiating with B&C, the Office of Fair Trading (OFT) produced a report that claimed that some undertakers were not abiding by the National Association's code of conduct. The OFT's survey, which covered only 900 respondents, suggested that one quarter had been given a price list to help them choose a funeral, and that two fifths had been given no price information at all. One third had not been given an estimate of the total cost, and another third had received only a verbal estimate. The *Independent* produced two widely differing articles on the subject on the same day. One article admitted that only 11% of the 892 people interviewed had expressed dissatisfaction with some part of the service, but claimed many had complained about price.

> Few people can bear to shop around; Trevor Dell of New Haw, Weybridge, Surrey, was an exception. His father asked him to find the cheapest possible funeral before he died. 'I was steeled by that to ring round about half a dozen undertakers, but they all quoted me similar prices of between £680 and £720 for the simplest funeral. Then I got an estimate of £350 from a local firm which did a very satisfactory job.'

On the City page, the *Independent's* financial staff enquired more closely and concluded that 'Much of the Office of Fair Trading's concern seems to be based on anecdotal evidence from a survey of 900 people. Although 11% said they were unhappy about parts of the service they received, only six people . . .complained about price, and the vast majority were completely satisfied.'

The three quoted funeral directors have always said that recommendation is extremely important to their businesses. Consequently the quality and price of the services they offer are of vital importance. At Hodgson Holdings for example, any complaints go straight through to chairman Howard Hodgson.

OFT was itself critical of the price of funerals, which had seen average rises of 28% above the rate of inflation in the twelve years to March 1987. However, that figure did not take into account disbursements to third parties whose share of the total cost has risen from 12 to 30% in that time. In recent years the three quoted groups' trading had shown that their charges had barely kept pace with inflation.

I was angry at the conclusions of the report and hit back hard telling the newspapers:

I don't understand the report. It contradicts itself in the space of a few sentences. And where they got the figures from I don't know. The criticism of price is totally unfair – that's exactly why we've had rationalization in this business because funerals don't cost enough. You show me a huge income per funeral market like Germany, Italy or Spain and I'll show you a very fragmented market. People do two or three funerals a month and survive. You show me a low funeral income market like the UK and I'll show you it's the most rationalized European market because the income is poor.

Sally Brompton of *The Times* looked into the report closely and questioned the major funeral directors. After giving space to some of the complaints highlighted by the survey, she put forth the counter-arguments of the funeral directors. She also pointed out that many funeral directors' costs were beyond their control. Typical disbursements might include £23 for the minister, £12 for the organist, £3–7 for the church heating, £50–60 for service sheets, £120 for the purchase of the grave, another £120 for the local cemetery charges, £100 for flowers and £40–50 for a notice in *The Times*. She noted that forty manhours are invested in every funeral, despite, according to me: 'the public's great misconception that making several hundred pounds is not bad for a couple of hours' work'.

In the end not much happened. The profession was very largely innocent of matters raised in an amateur report by the OFT. On the other hand if the National Association of Funeral Directors had ever vaguely done a reasonable PR job much of this criticism and even the report itself could have been avoided.

Earlier in the book I advised joining trade associations, for the reasons I gave. However, never expect too much of them. Never expect them to throw up people in your trade or profession that will do great things for it. Naturally there are exceptions. However, the vast majority of people who seek or receive high office, without pay, in such associations usually do so for personal glory and are often useless; they do it for personal gain and are therefore thinking of their company rather than the association, or because nobody else would take the job and although often nice people they are usually bloody ineffective.

The National Association of Funeral Directors was always rich in its abundance of all three categories. It had no vision, was a poor communicator with the general public and always seemed obsessed with internal politics. Nobody should be amazed by this as the whole profession while being extremely decent, honest and hardworking always damaged itself by its small-minded obsession with its local competitor. I never visited a funeral director in order to acquire him, without having to listen to the 'disgusting behaviour' of his competitor down the road for at least two hours before we could turn our attention to the business in hand – theirs. The vast majority of funeral directors are wonderful with their clients but if they bit their tongues while talking about their competition they would probably die from septicaemia. I suspect this is true of many trades or professions especially the more traditional ones that often lack commercial ability. Many funeral directors (certainly not all), I met had about as much chance of commercial success as Hartlepool United have of winning the F.A. Cup and it is this insecurity and lack of self-confidence that led them along with the either jokey or macabre image of this business, to break most of the rules stated earlier regarding jealousy, etc. As a result they are living proof of how important it is to keep such rules in your head.

Two interesting possibilities that in the end never happened came from my negotiations to raise extra capital during 1988 and the early part of 1989. If my negotiated deal with SCI in the United States had been concluded, it is most unlikely that the subsequent merger with Kenyon would have been possible. SCI wanted to buy in its own stock because of the falling price. As is often the case, the stock-market was perceptive, for SCI had a very difficult time in 1989. If I had got into bed with them we would have been sucked in, and would have been the first to be treated badly because we were not in the States. We would never have been able to do anything with PFG, and would not have been able to merge with Kenyon.

On the other hand, if Hodgson had not merged with Kenyon, it would have been facing the prospect of B&C or the liquidators of B&C (the company collapsed in early 1990) holding 20% of Hodgson equity. In the event, PFG insisted – quite correctly as it turned out – that B&C should be bought out; although this was due to the French company's fear of the powerful Gunn holding rather than crystal-ball gazing regarding the position of B&C.

As a final postscript to the launch of 'Dignity in Destiny', the tie-up with Colonial Mutual and the capitalization of brands, Hodgson Holdings moved up from the USM to a full listing in April 1989. It was hoped that the share price would benefit, as certain institutions, unable to invest in USM companies, could now become shareholders. The effect on the share price in fact was negligible, but nevertheless it was another step for the once tiny company conducting 400 funerals a year towards becoming a major public company.

Within two days we announced the acquisition of a further eleven companies for £2.6 million in cash; three in Scotland, three in the north of England, two in the east Midlands, two in the southwest, and one in the northwest. In total they added 2,200 to the group's annual funerals.

Two days later 'Bearbull' in the *Investors Chronicle* added Hodgson to his portfolio. The reasons were defensive. The British economy had severely overheated in 1988, and was now beginning to pay the price. The Chancellor of the Exchequer, Nigel Lawson, had not appreciated how strongly the economy was growing in 1987 and 1988, and had guessed the effects of the stock-market crash of 1987 wrongly. Mrs Thatcher had guessed more accurately, but Lawson – backed by British and American economists, the City, the financial press, and most Tories – felt confident enough to turn a deaf ear.

After the tax-reducing budget of 1987, the Tories swept back into power in the June general election, and the bull market roared on. At that stage, Mr Lawson clearly feared some overheating, and raised interest rates in August. This was totally unexpected in the market, and the *FT* 100 share index fell 100 points in a few minutes. It proved to be a mere hiccup, and the London market roared on along with New York, Tokyo, and all the other markets.

Then came the crash, and Lawson reacted by cutting interest rates sharply. He continued to do so right into spring 1988, trying to keep the pound below three deutschmarks, a level he felt necessary to keep British manufacturers competitive and to prevent recession. He continued his tax-cutting budgets, and in March 1988 simplified income tax into two bands – a standard rate of 25% and a higher rate of 40%.

In the real world, away from the stock-market, the British consumer – feeling prosperous thanks to generous earnings settlements, relatively low inflation, and a sharp rise in the price of his house fuelled by loose credit – was spending money like never before. By the middle of 1988 this expenditure showed itself in a series of balance-of-payments deficits that would have defied belief only a year or two earlier. In the year to March 1989 the total deficit in the UK balance of trade was £20 billion, or nearly

£2,000 million a month. (It was widely believed that one factor that cost Harold Wilson the 1970 election was the publication three days before the poll of a trade deficit of £57 million; by the late 1980s this was petty cash.)

Lawson's reaction was to switch from a policy of lowering interest rates to one of raising them – and sharply. From a low of 7.5% in the spring of 1988 the base rate was raised to 13% by the end of 1988. They were to continue up to 15% by autumn 1989, and to stay there for a year as the British consumer refused to stop spending.

To Mrs Thatcher's intense irritation, inflation rose too. The Tories had always asked the electorate to judge them on their record of inflation, and until 1988 it was a good one. After the bad start in 1979, thanks to the second oil price hike and the first Thatcher government honouring the Clegg Commission awards to say nothing of their nearly doubling the rate of VAT, the first Thatcher Administration had brought inflation tumbling to under 4% by the time of the 1983 general election, aided by high unemployment, a strong pound, and weak commodity prices.

There was a slight blip upwards in 1985, but a plunge in 1986 when the price of oil fell back almost to $5 a barrel (it had been $40 in 1980). However, the explosion of credit in the mid–1980s made it inevitable (and the Tories should have known it – they had after all campaigned on the platform of too much money causes inflation) that inflation would rise again. And it did. From the beginning of 1988 it rose inexorably. Mrs Thatcher blamed Lawson as she had always known pumping liquidity into the economy after the crash would cause inflation and Lawson blamed Mrs Thatcher for preventing him from taking the pound into the Exchange Rate Mechanism (ERM) of the European Monetary System (EMS), which would have effectively tied the British economy into a system controlled by the German Bundesbank and the deutschmark.

Independent from the German government, the Bundesbank enjoyed an enviable reputation for having control of the money supply, and therefore of inflation. For reasons best known to herself, Mrs Thatcher did not want to be tied to this successful system, but wanted to retain the independence to manipulate the British economy. Perhaps because having given way to Lawson once had meant not backing her own judgement and had been disastrous and perhaps because of her fear of 'slow power loss' from Westminster to Brussels. However, this independent manipulation had meant inflation in the past, and it was going to mean it now. By 14 April 1989 when 'Bearbull' bought Hodgson shares, he wrote:

> The impasse in the equity market had to break some time and in the event weight of bad economic news finally pushed prices downwards. With 2050 gone, the next support level on footsie should be around 2000

– and if that goes, we will be seeking a new bottom level for the 1989 trading range.

The origin of this deterioration is not hard to find. Since the last consumer spending figures, the easy assumption that the economy must be slowing has attracted widespread challenge. The jury, of course, is still out. But the market is beginning to ask what it will mean if 13 per cent base rates do not bring the economy to heel – and cannot take much comfort from the answers. Shock treatment – interest rates jacked up to 14 or even 15 per cent – may make recession inevitable. But even that may be preferable to the alternative of several years' crawling growth, high inflation and rising unemployment stretching out beyond the next election.

Despite this gloom, I was about to secure my biggest deal to date – a merger with, though some saw it as a takeover of – my rival, Kenyon Securities.

CHAPTER 8

THE CITY AND THE MEDIA

W hen dealing with the City, try to acclimatize quickly to its characteristics and behaviour patterns. Most people you will meet are intelligent and pleasant. While they are very good at judging businessmen, most of them would make poor businessmen themselves; you have nothing to be afraid of, and no need to have an inferiority complex. Use the City for what it is good at providing: advice, investors, and location. However, do not end up paying too much for these services, and never forget that the City exists because of commerce, not the other way round (the City occasionally makes that mistake itself, which remains one of its major defects).

INFORMATION

Information is important. Keep analysts, brokers and stockholders in-formed. Hold regular meetings. Use a good financial PR or investor relations firm to organize this programme for you, but do not pay them an outrageous retainer.

Whatever else, remember that it does not matter how well you are doing if the holders, potential holders, analysts, brokers, and so on do not know it. Many public company chief executives ignore this, but to do so is a professional failing.

Naturally, your client comes first and your staff second; if these people are happy then you will have a successful company, and therefore the stockholder will be happy. Your stockholder is the third important ingredient in the cake: not only does he own the company, but he has provided the investment by which you have satisfied your clients and provided jobs for your staff.

REALISM

Be realistic when making comments to institutions, brokers and analysts. Do not be over-pessimistic, which will cause you problems in the future when you want to create enthusiasm for the company. *Never* be over-optimistic, as missed targets or forecasts damage your credibility, and analysts who have to rely a lot of the time on what you tell them quite rightly hate to look stupid.

Be very wary of analysts who write for broking houses where your competitors happen to be corporate finance clients. Of course, they are supposed to be independently, accurately, and informatively writing for their clients, who happen to be the institutions. The pressures, however, are too great. Can you really imagine such an analyst recommending your company as a buy, while your competitor, who happens to be his employer's client, a sell? It is highly unlikely, and I can never remember it happening.

The conversation you have with the analyst always seems somehow to get back to your competitor. The City's famous 'Chinese walls' may not have bloody big holes, but they certainly do have cracks.

When making a presentation to the City, remember the following:

- Make it professional – use slides and other visual aids to make your point accurately and briefly.

- Use two or three directors. More is confusing, and less may look like a one-man show.

- Practise the presentation, especially who does what and who says what.

- Never let any of your directors ad-lib in a presentation. I once had a director who at a meeting of analysts forecast such an optimistic annual profit figure for the company that I nearly fell off my chair.

- Anticipate questions, practise who answers them, and what is said.

- Suffer fools gladly: you will be asked many stupid questions; answer them patiently and kindly.

Personally I was not always very good at obeying this last rule and remember one occasion in 1987 when indeed I had not been to bed for several days completing the Ingall's deal with the House of Fraser before the 2nd of May deadline. I had to immediately attend three very large institutional meetings to explain to them roughly what action I had taken, why I had taken it, and why it would be worth their while to buy the £17 million worth of extra stock I was issuing to complete the deal. At one of these meetings a very well respected and I might add normally intelligent institutional buyer asked me a question. I answered it. He then asked the same question. I answered it accurately, politely and indeed charmingly for a second time. He then asked the question for the third time and I looked at him and said, 'Well you may be right – I'm just the bloody idiot who runs this company.' Everyone laughed. I had been tired and allowed him to annoy me and as a result had destroyed him with a waspish one-liner. Although they had all laughed at his expense he could have become an enemy (happily he didn't) and the assembled company may never have felt so comfortable about the chief executive's behaviour again. Indeed a large stockholder complained to CCM (Hodgson Holding's brokers at the time) that he had just seen the side of Howard that he did not like and hoped in future presentations I would be returning to the boyish Paul McCartney-type presentation.

THE MEDIA

When I floated Hodgson Holdings in 1986, I was so concerned with how the media might handle the flotation of a funeral directing company that I did not wish to give any press interviews. After much discussion with the flotation team, and in particular the PR company, I agreed to have just one interview with John Jay, who was at the time a young journalist on the *Sunday Telegraph*. John then wrote a pre-launch article in which he treated the company most sensibly. The result was that Hodgson Holdings plc caught the media's imagination, and over the next four years the company was the subject of thirty-five television programmes, over one hundred radio interviews, and created more than one newspaper article per day.

Why did that happen? If we had been a computer software company, we hardly would have been noticed. It had a lot to do with the nature of the business, and the fact that, fortunately, my ability to improvise the odd one-liner delighted the media sometimes successfully and sometimes disastrously. Such flirtation with the media is attractive in a bull market with low gearing costs, and when you have a relatively small USM company it has tremendous advantages. When you become a fully listed company, and the market is bear and interest rates are high, a happy-go-lucky image can be dangerous. It is important to 'pro-act' the media rather than react to it. For most of Hodgson Holdings initial three years as a publicly quoted company it was reacting to the media rather than pro-acting. While everyone was envious of our media coverage, we were unable to manoeuvre our image into the position where we would have liked it to be by the time, as a fully listed company, we took on board the merger with Kenyon Securities plc.

Hodgson Holdings was also never able to capitalize on its publicity because the majority of its funeral directing companies were identified by their local names, and therefore the huge amount of free television time we received was of no consequence whatsoever. People were unable to identify Hodgson Holdings plc with the ground-floor company. The lessons to be drawn are obvious: have a controlled PR programme, and always try to attach it to the name of the product. A classic example is the way that Richard Branson has been able to promote his products so successfully in conjunction with the brand name Virgin.

There is some truth in the argument that all publicity is good publicity. I say 'some' as it is obviously not always true. 'Local Funeral Director buries wrong body' is not going to enhance that company's standing for example. However if you attempt to be too boring, contrite, and always want your publicity to emulate some free corporate video, then the media will ignore you. Publicity is important, and can be a useful form of free advertising.

JOURNALISTS

When talking to journalists, always be firm and steadfast in your beliefs, but never become rude and abusive. A little tenderness, kindness, or even discreet flirtation goes a long way. Journalists, like anyone else, love to be complimented and hate to be smashed into the ground. If you argue with a journalist, you may win the argument but ultimately lose the war, as he or she will express their irritation in an article, and, worse, their annoyance may continue for years and be reflected in future articles.

At the time of the launch of the pre-arrangement funeral plan 'Dignity in Destiny', a journalist from *The Times* came to a private early-morning press review that contained only six or so journalists. He was filmed for the BBC programme 'Dignity in Destiny', and stayed on to attend the official launch later that day at the Savoy. He then wrote two very kind articles in *The Times*, one under his own name about the year's profits of Hodgson Holdings, and the other under the 'Tempus' column concerning 'Dignity in Destiny'.

Someone, however, had neglected to put a new balance sheet in his press pack, and as a result he missed that we were going to adopt a controversial accounting policy concerning trade names. The next day the *Independent* and another paper led with this revelation. *The Times* City editor called the journalist into his office and asked him how he had managed to spend the whole day with me yet had failed to pick up this important point. The journalist got it into his head that this neglect was deliberate. The result was that he wrote a major *Times* article that criticized considerably the new accounting policy. He followed this with another article on the front page of *The Times* business section, criticizing 'Dignity in Destiny', quite inaccurately.

I had always enjoyed a marvellous relationship with the press until that point, and was hurt and upset by what seemed to be totally unwarranted attacks. I knew, however, that whatever the justification you could not react by going to war. I was very patient with the journalist over more than one lunch, and certainly arrested his desire to attack Hodgson Holdings in the press, even if I did not win back his confidence.

The British press love to build you up in order to knock you down. While by and large they have been very kind to me, and I have many friends, I have really had to work at it.

FINANCIAL VS FEATURE

There is a tremendous difference between the financial press and the feature press. The financial press prides itself on its tremendous accuracy. However 'pro' or 'anti', the facts must be correct. This is a commendable trait, and reflected in how their journalists behave at lunch: they eat little, drink little, and write a lot. They hardly ever seem to use tape recorders, I suppose because they must accurately record the information and translate it into an article within minutes of returning to their offices.

In comparison, the feature journalist tends to eat a lot, drink a lot, write little and record much. I have often felt they know exactly what they wish to write before the interview. Their stories are often more fun to read – but only when they are written about someone else.

Whether feature or financial, there is a mammoth difference between the tabloids and the broadsheets. Never expect the tabloids to produce an article you will be pleased with; on the other hand, as long as it is not too bad it does not seem to do any harm.

In general, do not get stressed about the press. What people read about you matters a lot less to them than it does to you, within a few minutes they have gone on to read something else and completely forgotten about the article. It is often a lot of fuss about nothing, and only in your mind.

TELEVISION

Initially, an appearance on television is a daunting prospect. They fall into four categories:

• The recorded interview in the studio (e.g., Susannah Simon's 'Business Daily' for Channel 4). Interviews tend to be short and about a specific subject, i.e. your interim results, and are thus easy to master quickly.

• The short story recorded at your offices (e.g., BBC2 'Money Programme'). These are time-consuming as they involve 'let's pretend' meetings, journeys in the car, and so on. On the other hand, if you cock-up the odd line, because they are not live, you can do the whole thing again.

• The fly-on-the-wall theory (e.g., BBC2 'Enterprise Culture'). These programmes are not at all time-consuming because you go about your normal working life and the camera simply follows you. You quickly forget it is there, so watch your language!

• The live television show (e.g., 'Central Weekend Live', 'Kilroy' or 'The Time and Place'). These are always nerve-racking before they begin. However, when the programme gets going, within a very few minutes you forget there are millions of people watching. They tend to be enjoyable, and the forty minutes seems to pass in about four seconds. Beware of accepting invitations to such programmes if the audience is rigged against you, or you are not going to get a fair hearing because by being there you will harm your company by appearing, rather than by not appearing.

Whatever the radio or television programme, always relax, be brief, be brave, and above all – be yourself.

I once asked a producer what he thought of a television interview I had done that morning and he replied, 'Marvellous, darling, but it was all Paul McCartney. Pity we never got to see the real you.' It was true – I had had flu and did not feel well and was very nervous. As a result I hid completely behind a Paul McCartney impersonation as I just didn't feel confident enough to get the real me out of the cupboard that morning and therefore had to rely on the old boyish role.

MY EXPERIENCE

The flotation in 1986 of a funeral directing company with a chief executive who looked most unlike the preconceived idea of what a funeral director looked like alerted the press and by 1987, prompted by the Ingall's deal publicity and the large *Sunday Times* colour supplement article by Michael Watts with its controversial photo by Barry Lewis, the press attention grew and spread from the financial to the feature pages, followed by the colour magazines, and the television and radio appearances started to become more frequent. Indeed to my amazement in 1987 I was asked to appear on television in one form or another about every three weeks. This was at the height of the bull market and certainly it seemed that entrepreneurs had replaced soccer players as bed-fellows of rock stars. Simon Preston vetted the invitations and gave the green light to most. He advised against three – a programme criticizing the ability of Nigel Lawson (I wanted to attend), one about being a sex symbol (I didn't want to attend) and one about a delightful old chap, Teddy Corbett-Winder, who wanted to do a DIY funeral (I wanted to attend and indeed overruled Simon to do so).

However, if we thought this was all very exciting it paled into a quiet life when compared to 1988. The combination of being presented to the Queen, included in *Who's Who* and in *Money* magazine's 200 Wealthiest People (the accuracy of this article I always felt to be dubious) above two Beatles and Miss Joan Collins among others kept the press busy. Adding Dennis Amiss to the team and making nearly 100 acquisitions during the year merely fuelled the fire. Naturally the headlines themselves seemed to be a source of amusement to most if not usually to me. Here is a small selection from 1988 – Body Shopping (*Daily Telegraph*), Pay Now Die Later (*Sunday Mirror*), Hodgson is Dying to Grow (*Today*), Nothing Funereal About Hodgson (*Financial Times*), Rising from the Grave (*Evening Standard*), Bodies Count (*Investors Chronicle*), Ashes to Ashes for Amiss (*Daily Mail*), It's All At the Co-op for Hodgson (*Investors Chronicle*), Symtactical Cricket (*Guardian*), Pennies from Heaven (*Business*), Firm Buries its Rivals (*Today*), Life After Death Service (*Daily Express*), Funeral Firm in Secret Deal with Unknown Body (*Guardian*), Undertaker is Overtaker (*Sunday Times*) and Howard Hodgson's Parlour Game (*Sunday Telegraph Magazine*).

In fairness there were well over 400 articles about either the company or myself during 1988 so quite a lot must have had sensible headlines. Moreover, given the nature of the business, most of the press had treated the subject sensibly even if that hadn't always been reflected in the headline. Anyway I should hardly keep going on about headlines when one considers the title of this book. Furthermore, they had been very kind to me and consistently backed me and my future image and plans for the profession against increasingly irritated and perhaps jealous competitors.

Many of the press had become friends and often gave me good advice. For example, John Jay told me – when I telephoned from Corcheval having performance on BBC2's Money Programme in 1987 was a huge mistake. It going on and on about Hodgson Holdings – 'Relax – they always talk about you. You always talk about you. Perhaps that's why you are always winning. You use 100% of your space for you. If they want to waste 50% of theirs on you too let them.' Very good advice.

At any level of competition do not let the opposition rattle you – be pleasant in public and work like hell in private to win. Colin Field's (son of Great Southern's Chairman and therefore a competitor) 'green with envy' performance on BBC2s Money Programme in 1987 was a huge mistake. It had been easy for me because I had won the day and the cameras were there to record my greatest deal to date, Ingall's. Michael Kenyon, Chairman of rivals Kenyon Securities, had lost but did his image no harm at all by behaving like a perfect gentleman. Field, in a poor media performance insisted that the House of Fraser had made a great deal as sellers of the business (therefore obviously implying that I hadn't). Not only did I in the next year prove him wrong, earnings per share rising from 6.6p to 11.6p – a perfect deal – but the next day everyone was saying 'who was that little jealous guy on "your" show last night'.

Television led to radio, radio led to the papers and the papers led to television and so on. Then came the French, German and Italian magazines and even one from Japan. However, none of us expected to be on the front page of the *Cape Times* in South Africa but we were. 'Hodgson Breathes Life Back Into Undertaking' was the headline and the article was a complete steal from the *Daily Telegraph*.

It was about this time that *Today* newspaper started to produce 'Hodgson Holdings cartoons' to accompany any news story about the firm. Many people in the funeral profession were outraged but actually I found them inoffensive and even funny.

The next year, 1989, continued in much the same vein. The launch of 'Dignity in Destiny', the BBC2 '40 Minutes Enterprise Culture' programme about the same and of course the takeover of Kenyon kept the press on its toes.

The *Radio Times*, understandably backing their programme, dedicated a whole page to a good interview with me under the typically silly banner 'Grave New World'. The BBC2 programme, a 'fly on the wall'-type production, made about the launch of the pre-arrangement scheme 'Dignity in Destiny' was then shown in June and reviewed the next day by nearly all the press. Everybody was great about the programme. Most were even great about Hodgson Holdings. The *Independent* even queried how I had managed to talk the BBC into making a corporate video for me. But then there was Peter Tory of the *Daily Express*. He seemed to like the programme, perhaps even the company, but he obviously hated me. I was described as vain, slick, arrogant and too clever for his liking. I was astonished, after three years of rewarded flirtation with the press, that here was someone being mean to me. I thought it unfair but I was most surprised by my 'couldn't care less' attitude to his comments. If they had been directed at the company or even the profession I would have been most upset but at me – well rightly or wrongly, I believed his comments to be wrong and as he had never met me he certainly couldn't be sure they were right. The PR firm St James and I thought it so far off the mark that we would quote it to each other and giggle. However the article sometimes popped up in later years and therefore proves that any 'anti' article, however silly, should be avoided.

The launch of 'Dignity' itself brought a landslide of press comments along with the usual crackpot headlines as of course did the merger with Kenyon. On both occasions we were racing against the clock to make it to the press conferences due to last-minute hold-ups with the solicitors or the Stock Exchange. The launch of 'Dignity' had been tight but the merger with Kenyon was impossible.

Michael Kenyon, most understandably due to the fact that he had not known about the merger until 72 hours earlier, was being awkward and causing delays while I had not been to bed for 48 hours. The conference had to be delayed due to Michael's refusal to agree the press release and without an agreed press release the information couldn't 'go on the Exchange screen'. If it wasn't 'on the screen' we couldn't hold the conference.

The Savoy, where the conference was to be held, promised to have a razor waiting for me that didn't materialize (this was needed as I hadn't shaved for two days). It was very hot and there was a rail strike on. Once the press release had been agreed, Sandy Fraser (UBS Phillips and Drew – Hodgson's new corporate advisers) and Michael Kenyon started to argue about the slides to be shown to the conference as Michael believed some showed Kenyon in a bad light. Sandy believed they were accurate and had to show how Hodgson was going to improve Kenyon's performance.

Meanwhile Simon Preston left a paper with the companies' code names (code names are always used to keep matters secret in advance of an announcement) lying around which was seized upon by Michael Walters of the *Daily Mail*. The names were Famine, Plague and Pestilence and led the next day to the *Mail's* headline 'Plague and Pestilence Put 19p on Hodgson'.

The press were getting more and more edgy as we hadn't started because unknown to them the 'damn' announcement still hadn't appeared on the screen. I said to Sandy Fraser, 'I am going to do it now, I'm not waiting any more.' He replied 'No, you can't, Howard, there is a guy over there with a portable phone and it's still not on the screen.' 'OK', I said, 'go and take the phone off him and if he won't give it take him behind that pillar, beat him up and then take it because I'm starting now.' And I did.

Michael Kenyon did his bit very well. I did the slide show. Philippe de Margery and Claude Pierre Brosolette of PFG, France's largest funeral director and Kenyon's major shareholder opened and closed the proceedings respectfully. Questions. The French were supposed to take the lead here to ease the Michael v Howard position. Remember what I wrote earlier about being prepared. They were not. Moreover they certainly were not prepared for the rudeness of a mass gathering of a tired and hot British press.

Michael Walters of the *Daily Mail* was leading the pack with his usual 'what worries me is'. I swung Brosolette's microphone over to me and interrupted 'what worries me is every time we meet you always start every sentence with "what worries me is" and you know if what worries you is the Hodgson valuation in this deal then perhaps if you hadn't spent most of the last three years describing me as either a Third Division footballer or ageing rock star then maybe the valuation would have been higher.'

The audience laughed and I slammed in 'next question – Ah, you – OK, stand up, please, and tell me your name'.

I quickly showed that I was not going to be intimidated by the large audience of journalists and analysts; I knew a lot more about the subject than they did and by getting them on their feet I was making it a one to one contest with me holding the knowledge and a pocket full of one liners. The questions became friendly, as did the press comment the next day. The French were impressed but totally shocked by British press behaviour.

The merger itself led to considerable French press coverage and our own press files became full of articles which most of my directors couldn't understand a word of.

Following the merger 1990 was a year for consolidation and therefore was quieter than '88 or '89. However the launch of the bereavement support service with Sir Harry Secombe and the National Training School caused much favourable press comment and as both were unrushed and orderly (unlike the merger) they were 'text book' affairs.

Dealing with the press is like skiing, sailing or batting – great fun as long as you get prepared properly before you start out. Moreover if you do, for whatever reason, get pushed into a corner, don't panic and always remember to be calm – you know a lot more and care a lot more about your company than ever the press will.

CHAPTER 9

THE REALLY BIG DEAL

If Ingall's had been a big deal in 1987, Kenyon Securities was a *really* big deal. Hodgson had been continuing to expand into the south, but to make any significant progress it had to buy, or merge with, one of the two public companies dominating the south of England – Great Southern Group or Kenyon Securities. Over the years I had had discussions with both on the possibilities of a tie-up, however it was Kenyon that increasingly had looked the more vulnerable.

Kenyon was founded in the 1820s. The firm was incorporated in 1870, and its first premises were in fashionable Kensington Church Street in west London. It expanded into other premises in Bishops Bridge Road, Paddington, and Westbourne Grove. Sir Harold Vaughan Kenyon, son of the founder, James Harold Kenyon, became a pillar of the Establishment, serving on the Kensington Borough Council, of which he became mayor, and on Paddington Borough Council, of which he also became mayor. He eventually became president of the Metropolitan Mayors' Association. He was knighted in 1937, and made his firm, J. H. Kenyon Ltd, the Establishment funeral director. In 1924 he built a block of flats near Marble Arch with offices on the ground floor. The head office was then transferred from Bishops Bridge Road to these offices. Until the Second World War the company had stables for the hearse horses in Connaught Mews, with the bearers and grooms living in flats above.

Sir Harold was succeeded by his son Norris, who followed in his father's footsteps by becoming deeply involved in local government. He also was knighted, in 1955. The company continued as a successful private company until 1970, when it was bought by a subsidiary of Gerrard and National Bank, Temple Securities.

This was the era of Slater–Walker and the go-go funds. Whereas equities on the London stock-market had been very dull in the 1930s and 1940s, and had only carried a higher yield than gilts because of the higher risk, by the 1950s, and certainly by the 1960s, the cult of the equity became established as businesses expanded in the post-war boom. Property prices, particularly in London, rose sharply, and shrewd operators realized that many companies were sitting on undervalued assets. Temple Securities saw Kenyon's valuable freehold properties, and bought the business for £1.3 million (about £10 million in 1991). They then split the company in two, exploiting the property and leaving the Kenyon family to run the funeral business.

When the bear market arrived in 1974, Gerrard and National were only too happy to sell the company back to the Kenyon family for £650,000. The company expanded slowly and steadily, and in 1983 was floated on the USM. Expansion continued, but as the 1980s progressed, two major rivals appeared: Hodgson Holdings and Great Southern. Kenyon was never as aggressive as the other two, but nevertheless appreciated that growth – obligatory for a public company – only would come in the static funeral industry through acquisition; it was therefore necessary for them to compete in the acquisition race.

It was an unequal contest. Hodgson performed far better financially, and that, linked to the publicity for Hodgson, had given Hodgson's share price such a boost that it was rated on a p/e ratio more than double Kenyon's. This gave me a distinct advantage. Kenyon also had turned down my offer of a joint deal over the purchase of Ingall's. Kenyon were further irritated by Hodgson's purchase of Ashton Ebbutt, as there was a family relationship between the two firms.

Growth comparison of the UK big three – pre merger						
(£m)	1984	1985	1986	1987	1988	Compound growth (%)
Turnover						
Great Southern	10.1	11.2	12.4	14.5	18.6	+16.5
Hodgson	1.5	1.9	2.7	8.3	17.8	+85.6
Kenyon	4.0	4.6	4.8	5.2	10.6	+27.6
Pre-tax profits						
Great Southern	1.31	1.42	1.77	2.29	3.0	+23
Hodgson	0.32	0.48	0.84	2.31	5.37	+102.4
Kenyon	0.41	0.43	0.75	0.85	1.63	+41.2
Earnings per share p						
Great Southern	9.1	9.5	14.2	15.2	19.0	+20.2
Hodgson	2.3	3.4	6.6	11.6	16.0	+62.4
Kenyon	8.4	8.1	11.5	12.1	12.5	+10.5

And I kept up the pressure. St James provided the newspaper and television interviews. I did not disappoint the readers and viewers. As the *Investors Chronicle* put it:

If Great Southern Group claims that it is constantly wooed by businesses wanting to come under its wing. Hodgson is more forthright – 'I don't know why funeral directors like to appear like blushing virgins. Of course we approach people.'

Hodgson wears swanky double-breasted suits, long hair and dark sunglasses. He professes to abhor the unctuous manner of the traditional undertaker and his conversation is far from lugubrious.... A recent profile in the *Sunday Times* – which labelled him as Mr Death – has confirmed him as the anti-hero of the funeral profession.

In a thinly disguised reference to the way Kenyon handled their takeover targets once they had acquired them I said: 'One of the lunatic things they [my fellow funeral directors] tend to say when they buy a business is that they're not going to change anything. If I were a shareholder I'd be mortified to hear that.'

During 1987 and 1988, all three companies, particularly Kenyon and Hodgson, were buying up small funeral directors as fast as they could. During 1987 I had several meetings with the directors of a substantial funeral company in north London, Dottridge Brothers. The family seemed to be moving smoothly towards a sale, and called in a merchant bank to give them advice. The merchant bank, not surprisingly, suggested they should talk to all three publicly quoted funeral directors, and Hodgson found themselves in an auction with Kenyon and Great Southern. Great Southern did not show much interest – I felt certain they would not borrow the necessary money – and the auction developed into a straight contest between Hodgson and Kenyon.

By this time – post-Crash 1987 – public companies were having to be much more careful about making acquisitions which might dilute their earnings-per-share, and I felt confident I could bid a higher price than Kenyon because all of Kenyon's recent acquisitions had been in the south against the competition of either Hodgson or Great Southern. They had therefore paid up to £1,500 per funeral on all their purchases, whereas Hodgson had paid only £700 for some of theirs in the north where the competition had been much less.

Hodgson bid £9.5 million for Dottridge's 5,700 funerals, and was confident it would be a higher bid than Kenyon's. I was right. But our joy was premature. The bid was, of course, subject to contract, and within a few days Hodgson received some extra demands: a BMW for a director; £50,000 a year salaries for him and the shareholding accountant; repayment of a £600,000 loan on top of the price for the equity; and a demand that we should pay Dottridge's merchant banking fees.

I was taken aback but was still keen to clinch the deal. What I did not know, but learned subsequently, was that Kenyon's persuaded the Dottridge directors to talk again to them. The result was that Hodgson were told they had not after all bought Dottridge, but that Kenyon had been the successful bidder.

Enormously irritated, I banged my fist on my desk and said, 'There will be no more champagne drunk in this office until Dottridge is part of this company.' Middleton, the finance director, pointed out that that would mean Hodgson would have to own Kenyon. 'So be it,' I said.

To mask my disappointment I went for a week's skiing, and received a telephone call from Graham Hodson that 'It's just flashed across the screens that Kenyon have just paid £11.5 million for Dottridge.' I could not believe it. I thought Dottridge had gone to Kenyon because they preferred them. Nevertheless, I was absolutely delighted. I knew that it was too much: Kenyon would suffer earnings dilution, which would not please any of their shareholders, and especially not their major shareholders the French firm PFG. I told Hodson that they would be ours within two years.

However PFG were not quite so quick witted, and they took the opportunity to increase their share of Kenyon from 10 to 28% in the placing Kenyon had to make to finance the deal. PFG was certainly a big brother, which had buried and cremated 235,000 French men and women in 1987 as well as manufacturing 230,000 coffins. It was also the biggest undertaker in Belgium, enjoyed 9% of the Swiss market, and for some odd reason 10% of the Singapore market. PFG was itself controlled by the Lyonnaise des Eaux group, with interests in water supply, heating, waste management, as well as funeral services.

The USM magazine made some interesting predictions following the increase in PFG's stake in Kenyon. Having analysed the reasons for PFG's interest in the UK in the first place – lower margins and a potential monopoly problem in France – it predicted:

It seems to us that the process of concentrating UK market shares into fewer hands is likely to continue for some time, probably at the current rate of acquisitions for two to three years. But conditions are going to get tougher, margins are probably going to reduce and access to finance is going to be less easy. Earnings per share growth in 1988/9 could also begin to slow. Kenyon via its tie-up with Pompes, would seem to have got the ideal solution although, because of the Takeover Code, Pompes cannot own more than 30% of Kenyon without triggering a bid. It is therefore going to be difficult for Kenyon to expand furthur via share placings without being vulnerable to a bid being triggered from Pompes. And Pompes would be very sensitive to any Francophobe slogans which the competition would be quick to produce. For these reasons investors should be alert to the possibility of a different sort of restructuring in the industry.

We would guess that in three year's time there will probably be only one quoted player left in the funerals business, possibly two. We see Kenyon being used as a takeover vehicle by Pompes and taking out either Hodgson or Great Southern or both.

Cleary the USM magazine did not know my personality too well. I had not come this far and shown greater skill and courage than Kenyon in every competitive situation to be taken out by them with or without PFG. In fact later in the article the writer had second thoughts:

> We believe a Pompes inspired Kenyon bid for Hodgson or even a Pompes inspired Hodgson bid for Kenyon is a distinct possibility. The logic for the French of 30% of a merged Hodgson/Kenyon business carrying out almost 50,000 funerals a year and probably run by the inspirational Howard Hodgson could be overwhelming.

Throughout 1988 I kept in touch with Herve Racine, PFG's finance director. At the same time I was talking to the largest funeral directing firm in the United States, SCI.

As all three of the quoted funeral directors absorbed more private companies and sought in their different ways to rationalize those they had bought, Kenyon felt the need to raise more money, and in September 1988 launched a rights issue to raise £6.7 million. Before the announcement, Kenyon's share price was 231p. The issue was deeply discounted at 150p and after the announcement the shares dropped to 218p and continued on down. The fact that the issue was underwritten, and not by PFG but by Lazards, seemed to suggest to the hopeful takeover speculators that PFG was not, after all, going to make a full bid. Clearly Kenyon was feeling the pressure. There were few really good independent funeral directors left, and the competition to buy them was keen, but Kenyon had shown little earnings-per-share growth for three years. In future they would have to pay cash; hence the need to replenish the coffers with a rights issue.

Conversations with PFG's finance director continued through the winter of 1988 into early 1989 – we had agreed a plan in the summer of 1988 which had been scuppered by the Kenyon board – but, as we have seen, were affected, at least on my side, by the launch of 'Dignity in Destiny' and the financial deal with British & Commonwealth. It was clear to Hodgson that all was not well in the Kenyon camp. There were reports of constant boardroom rows, and a poor middle management with no great commitment to the work ethic.

I kept talking, and finally in July 1989 a deal was struck. The *Independent* summed up the situation accurately:

> The merger between funeral director Hodgson Holdings and Kenyon Securities seems to give all the parties what they want. Howard Hodgson becomes chief executive of Britain's largest funeral director chain; the French group Pompes Funebres Generales swaps a 28% stake of Kenyon for 25% of the enlarged group, PFG Hodgson Kenyon International; and Michael Kenyon gets a retirement nest egg and a non-executive directorship.

It also pointed out, correctly, that it was clear that Hodgson and PFG had hatched the deal and presented Kenyon with a *fait accompli*, and also pointed out, again correctly, that Michael Kenyon was probably unhappy having his company tied in with Hodgson.

> Mr Kenyon has never made a secret of his dislike of Hodgson's way of doing business. Both groups, in common with the other quoted funeral director, Great Southern Group, have been expanding aggressively in recent years, buying up independent outlets. Mr Kenyon has often said the directors who sell to him would not have considered joining Hodgson. Now these directors have been sold to the company they rejected lock, stock and barrel.

The logic of the deal, however, was inescapable. The total market was flat, even declining, and would be for another ten years. Funeral prices had not risen, and were still not rising, as fast as inflation. Over 80% of the cost of funerals were fixed, and therefore the attractions of economies of scale were overwhelming.

The *Guardian*, as with so much of the media, seemed incapable of being wholly serious about anything to do with funerals:

> The architects of the deal presented a varied picture at yesterday's slightly less than smooth-running formal ceremonies. Claude Pierre-Brosolette,

who will be chairman of the new company, is a former head of France's Treasury department and served as President Giscard d'Estaing's chief of administrative staff. Flanking him was Hodgson Holding's chairman, Howard Hodgson, whose youth and near shoulder length blond locks have seen him compared with a fourth division footballer ...Kenyon Securities chairman, Michael Kenyon, was unsurprisingly, puzzling as to whether his description as 'a middle aged, retiring man, very much the popular image of the undertaker' was flattering or not.

SOME PROBLEMS AND A GRAND ALLIANCE

As with all major takeovers and mergers, not all shareholders were happy. The French company was believed to have insisted on a one-for-one deal in the shares between Hodgson and Kenyon. Some of the Hodgson shareholders who had subscribed two years earlier for shares in Hodgson at 240p were not happy with the 180p at which the two were going to be merged. And when Kenyon's latest results were announced on 26 July *The Times* highlighted further objections:

Kenyon Securities has produced disappointing results for the year to end-March with earnings per share dropping 7 per cent to 10.8p. The decline makes the merger terms look increasingly unbalanced. Several Hodgson shareholders are suggesting they may oppose the deal when the offer document is published ...Kenyon says its poor performance is a result of a fall in the death rate in the south of England where it has most of its branches.

These results, however, contrast sharply with Hodgson Holdings' interim figures, announced with the merger last week, which showed earnings up 13 per cent to 9.3p. Yet Hodgson and Kenyon shareholders are being offered the same one-for-one share swap in the merged company, PHK International, with a part cash alternative at 180p. The terms value Hodgson at less than 11 times historic earnings, but Kenyon at more than 16. It is believed the one-for-one terms were insisted on by Pompes Funebres Generales which holds a 29% stake in Kenyon and is taking a 25% stake in PHKI.

However there were few problems in the boardroom as Michael Kenyon, despite a prickly start, became a friend and ally and often supported me strongly against some of the more silly ideas from the French. Moreover I came to realize that he resented the French much more for giving his company away than he did me for wanting to run it. Furthermore, I, now nearly 40, still missing my father, who had died 5 years previously, was happy to look to him and ask his advice and almost adopt him as a father figure. Michael wasn't always very sensible but then neither was my father and for that matter who is? Mostly you have to get there on your own.

After the hectic expansion of the three previous years, when Hodgson and Kenyon had been buying as many independent funeral directors as they could – sometimes without checking thoroughly enough whether they were worth the price being paid – there clearly needed to be a period of consolidation. Apart from their own internal management considerations, the general economic and stock-market climate was not conducive to further headlong expansion. The British economy was taking longer to respond to high interest rates than anticipated, and in autumn 1989 the smouldering row between Margaret Thatcher and Chancellor Nigel Lawson, ended in his resignation and replacement by John Major. Major continued the regime of high interest rates, and for business the issue became one of survival, not expansion.

PFG Hodgson Kenyon International, or PHKI, in one way was ideally suited to such conditions – people do not stop dying because interest rates are high. On the other hand, as we have seen, in such a static market, Hodgson and Kenyon only had secured growth through acquisition and rationalization of the firms acquired. For the moment, further acquisitions would be limited. And although people would continue to die, their relatives probably would spend less on their funerals. Thus, the best prospects for the group would come from further rationalization, such as the sale of surplus hearses and the negotiation of better terms for the purchase of coffins and gowns, and from the extra contribution from additional services such as floral, monumental and limousine hire.

In early 1990 financial commentators were fairly if not euphorically bullish. The *Investors Chronicle* Stockmarket Letter wrote: 'The shares have considerable long-term growth potential and should be bought.' County Nat West was a little more macabre: 'We have raised our forecast for 1990 from £13.32 million to £14.5 million because of a surge in the death rate in January which has got the year off to a good start.'

The ICI Stockmarket Letter picked this up and under the heading 'signs of a good start to 1990' and noting that Great Southern in its recent report had said: 'Trading levels since December 1989 have increased significantly' continued to recommend PHKI as offering 'strong defensive characteristics and long-term growth potential'.

The merger with Kenyon was a logical development for Hodgson. Nevertheless, it had taken courage, skill, and foresight to push it through, particularly in the light of gradually worsening economic and stock-market conditions.

Throughout this book the theme, concerning funerals, has been a static death rate and growth for funeral companies only through acquisition. What are the prospects for the future of PHKI? A stable, sluggish performance, conducting 65,000 funerals efficiently each year, with all the excitement of the 1980s a fading memory? Or further dramatic growth and drama in the 1990s? Andrew Yeo, an analyst at stockbrokers, UBS Phillips, saw it differently: 'Now it's all about added value.' At the end of 1989 he wrote:

> PHKI offers investors the opportunity to hedge against recessionary pressures in the economy whilst benefitting from the Hodgson/Kenyon merger which we expect to produce operational cost savings of £2 million a year. In the long term, the development of ancillary income from pre-paid funeral plans and monumental masonry will ensure strong earnings growth moving into the 1990s.

The development of 'Dignity in Destiny' and of post-funeral financial services will be a gradually accelerating generator of profit in the 1990s. 'Dignity' not only generates additional profit, but will guarantee future market share and enhance the company image. With a good percentage of the population over forty-five, and therefore likely to be interested in considering a pre-arrangement plan, the growth that started in 1986 will continue through the 1990s and into the next century. (The death rate will remain stable until the end of the century, but will then grow steadily.)

It is important for PHKI in the future to focus on organic growth. Not just financial organic growth through its ancillary income, but the organic growth of its market share by branding its service. Much of management's effort and the shareholders' money has been put into providing excellent and uniform standards of service and facility. All PHKI hearses and limousines are now midnight blue Volvos. All office staff have uniform midnight blue livery while that of the chauffeurs is portland grey. There is an expensive capital investment programme afoot to convert all funeral homes and branch offices to the same uniform corporate colours. The introduction of a brand name is essential, as the cornerstone of this investment programme and the route to organic market share growth.

The realization that a branded image was necessary for the future came in 1987. It was due to Hodgson Holding's typical attention to detail and its appreciation that a national chain must have equipment of the highest quality that the Volvo deal was struck. The catalyst for the deal was that I was told I could no longer expect 15% discounts on the Ford Dorchesters we had been using. In future I would receive a lower discount, and only be able to take one vehicle in part exchange for every new vehicle.

This prompted me to talk to Volvo, as I had felt for some time that the Volvo 740, as it was box- rather than wedge-shaped, would look attractive as a limousine. In the autumn of 1987 I flew to Sweden to buy 127 Volvos, replacing my whole fleet. Volvo chose a British company, Glenfrome Engineering, famous for their Range Rover conversions, to carry out the necessary conversion work. The value of the order was £4 million and Glenfrome agreed to take 150 vehicles in part exchange for £2 million.

Having taken care of how our funerals looked, we turned our attention to making sure our staff was second to none in the service they offered. In the long term we knew that consistency of good service could only be achieved by one thing: effective and continuous training. We set up the Acorn training programme.

At the opening of the Imperial Training Centre, it was emphasized that training was now a must, and no longer something it would be nice to have. To progress, PHKI must have an improved rate of referrals, and increased sale of peripherals, a better service to its clients, and a lower turnover of staff. For the company's 400 branches and 1,500 employees, better training was the only way. The *Guardian* summed up the launch, and showed it was not only PHKI employees who would benefit:

> The funeral industry yesterday laid to rest its heritage of spasmodic preparation for eternal farewells by unveiling its first comprehensive training package, covering everything from coffin presentation to the 'dos and don'ts of the flip chart'. Courses will be offered initially to the 1,500 employees of PHK International, which has invested £500,000 in an open-learning plan where students advance at their own – in this case respectful – pace. By January 1991 the whole industry is expected to be able to benefit from courses and eight supporting seminars. These include 'a fascinating day that explores the Monumental Memorial Service'; advice on presenting 'the full range of coffins in a professional and caring manner' and discussion about 'hygienic treatment, and what should we tell the client?'

In January 1990 the launch of a bereavement support service under the auspices of PHKI received a huge welcome from the media, helped by Michael Kenyon's brilliant idea of co-opting the popular comedian and former 'Goon', Sir Harry Secombe.

I had personal experience of the need for counselling at the time of a bereavement. In 1982 I had lost my three-year-old son, Charles, and had tried to adopt the typical British, do-not-show-any-emotion approach. A few years later I commented in a Radio 4 programme on bereavement:

> Nobody really expresses their grief. It's part of the middle class attitude, keep a stiff upper lip and pretend it hasn't happened. This is very damaging to the individual. It's important to express grief and let it out.

Although I knew all that, when I lost a son I reverted completely to type. Stiff upper lip, show must go on, et cetera, and I was actually quite incapable of coming to terms with it. Whereas my wife, Marianne, who is a French Roman Catholic, was terribly grief stricken at the time and as a result started to recover much more quickly. And everyone, of course, was saying, 'Isn't Howard wonderful, hasn't he been marvellous and wasn't Marianne lucky to have him' when really the reverse was true. She had actually come to terms with it while I was sitting at home at night looking at the walls like a zombie.

In the end I recovered enough to set up the Charles Hodgson Foundation for Children, which raises money for children's hospitals, and I was more than happy to support a bereavement telephone helpline. The service was compiled after consulting solicitors, funeral directors, the department of social security and voluntary groups such as Cruse Bereavement Care, a national organization set up to provide practical and emotional support for the bereaved. There was advice on eleven topics, all taped by Sir Harry Secombe. Each subject could be dialled on a separate number and lasted about three minutes, with calls being charged at normal British Telecom peak and off-peak rates. PHKI would take no profit from the calls, and a percentage would be donated to the charity Help the Aged. To promote the service, PHKI offered a free leaflet from its own branches and from various public places such as libraries. At the launch Sir Harry said – after making a crack about using the service himself because of a bad dose of flu: 'When anyone suffers a bereavement they feel so numbed that they often can't think straight. To be able to make a simple phone call and find a friendly, familiar voice at the end of it, able to offer sound advice, can only be of help.'

The subjects on the tapes included:

- Making a will

- Planning your immediate money matters on death

- The cost of funerals

- Pre-payment funeral and memorial plans

- What to do in the event of death; in the home; in a nursing home or hospital, etc.

- What to do in the event of a sudden or unexpected death

- Arranging a funeral

- Assistance with paying for a funeral

- Coping with bereavement

- What to do if a relative dies without a will

With training, care, and support for such praiseworthy ventures as the Bereavement Support Services, we had shown we understood the need for the national company to be as personally involved as the local, traditional funeral director. The national company can give the personal service, usually will be more efficient, and invests more in better capital equipment.

In 1990 we could not have expanded greatly by acquisition due to the economy, the market, and our own gearing position. We did not want to anyway, as getting the new company PHKI under control in an industry with no management history was a big enough job. Perhaps a boring year media-wise, but one the company will be pleased with in future years.

Did I enjoy it? No, I hated it. But I had led my shareholders and staff into the merger, and therefore owed it to them to put my head down, roll up my sleeves and make the deal, and therefore the new company, work.

Thanks to the market and the cost of gearing, our remaining competitors – Great Southern, and the Co-op had to slow down as well; it is much easier to take a breather when the other runners are having to also.

You must always make decisions that are in the long-term interest of your stockholder, and not be over worried or influenced by the activity of your competitors. Hodgson only worried about itself and the profession as a whole. It got some things wrong, but most right in a dazzling decade when it rose from nowhere to dominate, and probably change forever, an industry that had hardly moved in a century. Not many companies have done this, and to achieve it in a cottage industry with no on-tap management or reasonable capital base is a major achievement.

Great Southern, while more pedestrian, less adventurous and inventive, never became dazzled – sometimes irritated but never dazzled – by Hodgson. If Hodgson was revolutionary, then Great Southern was evolutionary and thus remains a company that I admire, even though I am always a little worried about 'evolution' as it often means 'do not do anything and see what happens'. Kenyon tried to imitate rather than 'do its own thing' and lost. There is a lesson here for all of us.

CHAPTER 10

FUTURE PERFECT?

At the beginning of 1991, every financial commentator was predicting much more difficult trading circumstances than were experienced for most of the 1980s. Their prophecies of gloom differed only in their forecasts of how long the misery would last.

Some pundits expect the new Prime Minister John Major and his new Chancellor of the Exchequer Norman Lamont, to give way to the calls for a reduction in interest rates in view of the electoral cycle, a cycle that has served British economic management so badly. Others expect them to resist, trusting Major to stick to his word that he will defeat inflation. His credibility was damaged when he reduced interest rates when Britain joined the Exchange Rate Mechanism of the European Monetary System in October 1990. They saw it as a clear political move, and were reinforced in their belief by the governor of the Bank of England letting it be known that he would not have reduced rates at that time.

Reduction or not, life will be more difficult than in the halcyon days of 1982–87. And what of Mrs Thatcher's influence? This is not a book about her (or at least it is not supposed to be) but its original inspiration was to write about the experiences of a successful businessman who was unknown when she came to power but who was a nationally known figure at the end of her first decade of rule (little did we know that within a year of conceiving the idea of the book she would be forced to resign by her colleagues who feared she had become an electoral liability).

Many millions of words have already been written about Margaret Thatcher and Thatcherism. The question is whether I would have achieved what I did under another government or would Hodgson and Sons still be a Birmingham funeral director. Nothing of course is certain and we do not know what would have happened if first, Margaret Thatcher had not been elected to the leadership of the Conservative Party in February 1975, and secondly, what would have happened if Callaghan had called a General Election in the autumn of 1978 instead of waiting until after the Winter of Discontent.

We can surmise that the Labour Government might have continued with their tight public expenditure policy of the late seventies – many believe that the Thatcher government introduced constraints on public expenditure. In fact they were introduced – imposed is perhaps a better word – in 1976 after the visit of the men from the IMF. If so, they may well have created some of the conditions that allowed the upswing in business that occurred in the mid–1980s. In any event, the upswing was worldwide and would have happened irrespect've of the colour of the British government.

What we can say with certainty is that Margaret Thatcher captured the mood of the majority of the people – though she never received anywhere near 50% of the votes of the electorate – who wanted a change from the bad old days of shoddy service from nationalized industries and bullying from powerful unions. She was a lucky Prime Minister and good luck brought her General Galtieri when she needed an enemy to beat to show the world neither she nor her country was a pushover. Good luck to bring an economic cycle so that the price of commodities, especially oil, plunged to give the Western world a long non-inflationary economic boom. Finally, good luck brought her another enemy to beat at home, Arthur Scargill, so that she could prove that supposedly invincible unions could be faced down and defeated.

However she rode her luck and was prepared to stick to her principles even when surrounded by doubters, compromisers and consolidators. Others would have benefitted from the benign conditions of the mid–1980s but it would probably only have been to the extent that they had done in previous upswings of the world economy, i.e., limited growth but still relative decline. Under Thatcher many more were able to benefit and to push Britain along on a path of faster growth and relative success.

Was my success totally dependent on *her* success? I hope I am an able businessman, Mrs Thatcher or no Mrs Thatcher. When I bought my father's nearly defunct company in 1975 she had only just been elected leader of the Conservative Party, and was four years away from being Prime Minister. It was during those four years that I laid the foundations of what was to become a successful public company. I had begun my growth-by-acquisition policy before Margaret Thatcher came to power.

Nevertheless, my progress would have been more pedestrian without the stock-market conditions created by the Thatcher Government's policy in the mid–1980s. Without the backing of my expensive paper – and part of the reason my paper was expensive was that many businessmen in Britain in the eighties were no longer shy and retiring types, they were hyped up and their share price with them – I could not have progressed as quickly as I did. With my own shares on multiples in the 40s and 50s I was able to swallow others on multiples in single figure thus further enhancing my own earnings per share and consequently my share price. No bank would have lent me the money to buy Ingall's for £17.5 million if I had still been a private company. And as successful deal followed successful deal I came to the notice of the rich and powerful. I was able to turn to John Gunn when others were wavering and I was able to convince the large French company, Pompes Funebres Generales that I was the man to back in the major rationalization of the funeral industry.

So perhaps we can say I would have built a major company with or without the Thatcher Years, but that it would have been a slower and longer process. With or without Mrs Thatcher I was always going to be a successful businessman, and my rationalization of the industry was made possible just as much by conditions she came to eradicate – inflation, sloppy management, and militant unions – as by the conditions she tried to create – low inflation, efficient, well-rewarded management, and constructive unions. So what does the future hold for PHKI, Mrs Thatcher, you, and me?

I predict that PHKI will remain a major force in funeral directing in the UK. How major will depend on its courage. If it takes on board branding, then very major; if it does not, then major, but less major than it is today, especially if it does not have the capital available to acquire. Branding would not only be cheaper in the short term, but more sustainable over the long. Either way, 'Dignity in Destiny' will be a powerful source of business and profit as long as it is run correctly. The ties with the French will get stronger, but I doubt if they will bid for the company, especially in the short term. The company must look for strong management and it will not find it in the ranks of the funeral profession.

I hope that Margaret Thatcher will continue to tour the world lecturing and receiving the acclaim that is heaped upon her wherever she goes. From Russia to the USA, from Japan to Canada and so on she is a heroine. A world super star who is still young enough to enjoy the accolades of her success without the pressure of having to perform in the future. I hope she is offered and takes a job at either the United Nations or Nato or some other suitable post. I hope she will not, but rather fear she will, interfere with government, especially over the European issue. She would do this out of deep conviction rather than Edward Heath's peevish objections to everything she ever did. However it would be a massive mistake and most unhelpful to her party, the government, the country and herself – in fact most of what she holds dear.

With no Margaret to protect it – should Thatcherism be allowed to fade away. I certainly hope not – as we have seen before Thatcher and Thatcherism the country stumbled from sterling crisis to sterling crisis led by men who totally failed to control militant unions or create a climate whereby we, the people, had the incentive to save ourselves.

The Germans laughed at our 'tea and strikes' while the rest of the world described us as 'the sick man of Europe'. We were in such a state that we decided to buy what seemed at the time the bitter pill of Thatcherism as a cure. We were ready. We hadn't been ready in the sixties. Did it provide a cure?

It dealt with the unions and for that matter with many restrictive practices closer to the Tory ranks – Big Bang, the Financial Services Act, opticians, etc., etc. It got rid of many of the large nationalized monopolies that were often a drain on taxpayers' money, allowed the people *really* to own them by owning shares in them and often ensured, by privatization, that the services given or products made (British Airways and Jaguar are notable examples) dramatically improved.

Despite Nigel Lawson, who broke its rules, its record on inflation is better than previous governments. It understood that governments don't run economies, they only create the conditions by which commerce and the people do. By controlling inflation it hoped to create the conditions, by lowering taxes it hoped to create the incentive for all to have a 'go'. It allowed people to earn more, save more and have more freedom on what they spent their money on. It believed in the individual and the family and not the State. It realized you have to create wealth before you could spend it. It gave management back the right to manage as the best way to create such wealth and it provided BES schemes, the third market and the USM as stepping stones to get there. It wasn't its fault if some people, 'mind blown' by the opportunity and drunk with the success of the eighties, overstepped the mark. Moreover for everyone who failed many more succeeded and at least, we were trying and being positive as a nation rather than cowering before bullying unions.

In giving most people middle class aspirations it did more to rid the nation of its old fashioned class structure and despite its hard image it managed to spend more on things like the health service in real terms than previous Labour or Tory administrations.

Its success can be measured by how far it has moved Labour policy to the right. Official Labour policy now stands to the right of the last Heath Conservative government – not bad for a Party that seemed obsessed with gay liberation rights for lesbians in Lambeth a decade ago.

The world is rejecting old fashioned senile, non-productive socialism as it rejected feudalism before. Do we really want to step back to those days as Eastern Europe steps forward? Much of Thatcherism is just good common sense. At times tough but then so is life and when the going gets tough the tough get going.

Common sense should not go out of fashion and Thatcherism should not disappear just because Margaret Thatcher has. Moreover, I don't think it will. John Major may appear to be a softer and more gentle political leader but his Citizens' Charter seems to me to be right up Mrs Thatcher's street and that's Thatcherism.

Furthermore, if you want to succeed in business you need policies that are in line with her philosophy or would you prefer a return to higher personal and corporate taxes and secondary picketing.

As for me, on 18 January 1991 I retired from the funeral directing profession. I sold my stock in PHKI to PFG, and resigned as chief executive. There followed much speculation by the press as to why I had, and the market totally overreacted, with shares tumbling from 128p to 68p within days. Did I not like the French? Had I argued with the French? Was there something wrong with either the company's, or my own, health?

The market and the press could not understand why a man who had built an empire and changed a profession (at times almost single-handedly) could turn his back on it all. People just do not do those sort of things. Well I did, and this is why.

For a long time I had always wanted an exit. I loved the company and was proud of what I had built, but I had three huge problems: I never saw my family: all the wealth was tied up in Hodgson Holdings' stock, of which I dared not sell a slice (remember what happened when I did); and, most important of all, I did not want to be remembered as the *enfant terrible* of funeral directing. I had other goals to achieve and a successful exit was the first.

A major attraction to me personally in doing the deal with the French was that it gave me an exit. I did not exercise this idea until I had stayed long enough to make the merger successful. I was loyal to the stockholders. But I always knew there would come a time when I must be loyal to my family and to myself.

In November 1990 I was in hospital suffering from disc trouble, which eventually led to an operation. I thought to myself, Howard you are forty. If you don't go now, you'll never go. Is that what you really want? I really did not want to mind the shop for the next five years. I did not believe over that period I could do much for the company, due to the economic recession, except mind the shop, and therefore would be totally bored.

Moreover, I was very tired. Fifteen years spent building a large public company out of a cottage industry that had no natural management had been a long slog. I had made several million pounds and was financially secure. Now I wanted to do what *I* wanted to do. I was very proud of the Hodgson & Sons/Hodgson Holdings/PHKI saga, but now was the time to end the story. And that is exactly what I did.

You may wish to exit – i.e. sell up – for similar or for entirely different reasons to me. Either way your exit is a very important deal – perhaps the most important deal as it is your last with that company. Get it wrong and there is no way back. You don't want to wake up a week on Wednesday thinking what a bad deal you made. Moreover it is highly likely that you will have to face an exit at some point unless you have a son or daughter that wishes to follow you (and is good enough) or you intend to die at your desk without much regard for your company or your family.

All the points I made earlier in the book concerning deal making apply to exit, especially those concerning planning in advance, not getting boxed in and not appearing too eager. When PFG kindly agreed to buy my shares I was delighted but I kept calm and excused myself to go to the loo where I smashed my fist into the air saying 'Yes, Yes, Yes'. However while taking a pee I gave myself a good talking to and reminded myself that I could only do this deal once and I had better get it right. The result was that I walked away £800,000 richer than if I had been too eager to start with. Many people made money in the '80s. Fewer kept it. I kept mine and knowing when and how to exit was why.

Exit, especially at an older age, becomes easier to achieve if you have a good pension lined up. You are much more likely to dictate timing and terms if you are not worried by future income considerations. Start a pension now and fund it well over the years.

I now do what I want to, working with HRH the Prince of Wales on the Prince's Trust, and I have four careers. Writing is one; I work as a presenter for the BBC, I have opened a business development company with my good friend John Gunn and I have launched Hodgson Securities plc.

And what about you? Could you do it? While I bet you have the capability, do you have the discipline or staying power. We started with inner conviction, and that is where we finish. *That* is what makes the difference. If you possess it, you will achieve; if you do not, you will not.

There are big prizes to be won. The cost of gearing will come down and the bull market will return. Admittedly we still have to worry about our poor attitude to the European Single Market, the possible follies that could arrive with a change of government; the upheaveal in Eastern Europe, the catastrophic state of world banking and the effect of a Japanese economic dose of flu. Is it going to be worth the hard work? I think so.

Hodgson Securites burst into the media in October 1991 and attracted over 40 articles including most of the major nationals. Prontac in particular caught the headlines and received excellent reviews all round.

Why did this new company get such coverage? Because of me. Why did I let my name attract so much publicity so early on in its life? Because I knew it would be successful and even more so because of the effect the publicicity would have both internally and externally. This has proved to be the case. On the other hand you could ask what if the reviews had been bad? I never thought they would be. Why should they be? We have a good product range and work hard. I said at the time of the launch, 'I don't think anyone has ever taken two different companies in two different fields from scratch and floated them on the Unlisted Securities Market. I intend to prove that it can be done in the next 3 to 5 years.' I will. And over this period what will you be doing?

Some Useful Addresses

Business in the Community,
    227a City Road, London EC1V 1LX – 071-253-3716
British Institute of Management,
    2 Savoy Court, London WC2R 0EZ – 071-497-0580
    Management House, Cottingham Road, Corby,
    Northants NN17 1TT – 0536-204222
Association of Independent Businesses,
    Ilford House, 133-5 Oxford Street, London W1R 1TD – 071-792-9776
National Federation of Self-employed and Small Businesses Ltd,
    32 St Anne's Rd West, Lytham St Annes, Lancashire FY8 1NY – 0253-720911
Small Business Bureau,
    46 Westminster Palace Gardens, Artillery Row,
    London SW1P 1RR – 071-976-7262
British Franchise Association,
    75a Bell St, Henley-on-Thames, Oxon RG9 2BD – 0491-578049
Companies Registration Office,
    Companies House, Crown Way, Maindy,
    Cardiff CF4 3UZ – 0222-388588 (England and Wales)
    102 George Street, Edinburgh EH2 3DI – 031-225-5774 (Scotland)
    also for those in the south of England:
    Companies House, 55 City Road, London EC1Y 1BB – 071-253-9393
Department of Trade and Industry Consultancy Initiative – contact your local office or
    for the Enterprise Initiative dial 100 and ask for Freefone Enterprise.

BIBLIOGRAPHY

BOOKS FOR NEW BUSINESSES

Abbot, M., *Small Business Handbook*, Hallmark, London, 1989

Barrow, C., *The New Small Business Guide*, BBC Books, London, 1989

Burstiner, I., *The Small Business Handbook: A Comprehensive Guide to Starting and Running Your Own Business*, Prentice-Hall Press, Englewood Cliffs, NJ, 1989

Cohen, W.A., *The Entrepreneur and Small Business Financial Problem Solver*, Wiley, New York, 1989

Consumers Association, *Starting Your Own Business*, Consumers Association, London, 1989

Deschampsneufs, Henry, *Export for the Small Business*, Kogan Page, London, 1988

Dudley, Jim, *How to Promote Your Own Business*, Kogan Page, London, 1988

Earls, G., and Forsyth, P., *Making Marketing Work*, Kogan Page, London, 1989

Franks, Ray, *Commonsense Computer Management: A Practical Guide for the Non-professional*, Kogan Page/Chartered Institute of Management Accountants, London, 1989

Glen, G.R., *The Small Business Financial Planner*, Wiley, New York, 1989

Gorton, K., and Doole, I., *Low Cost Marketing Research: A Guide for Small Businesses*, Wiley, New York, 1989

Kenny, B., and Dyson, K., *Marketing in Small Business*, Routledge Kegan Paul, London, 1989

Lewis, Christopher, *Employee Selection*, Hutchinson, London, 1985

Lewis Brown, J., and Howard, Leslie R., *Principles and Practice of Management Accountancy*, Macdonald and Evans, London, 1975

Mohr, Nicholas, *Distribution for the Small Business*, Kogan Page, London, 1990

Ordidge, P.D., *Simple Cash Books for Small Businesses*, Kogan Page, London, 1989

Patten, D., *Successful Marketing for the Small Business*, Daily Telegraph Guide, Kogan Page, London, 1989

Sewell, Ron, *Building a Business*, Pan, London, 1987

Stone, Norman, *How to Manage Public Relations: Practical Guidelines for Effective PR Management*, McGraw-Hill, London, 1991

Turner, P.H., and Voysey, P., *Start Your Own Business*, Blandford, London, 1989

Whitehead, G., *Bookkeeping and Accounting*, Pitman, London, 1989

Wilmshurst, John, *The Fundamentals and Practice of Marketing*, Butterworth-Heinemann, Oxford, 1991

Winters, Chartered Accountants, *Being a Director: A Guide to the Responsibilities and Opportunities*, Kogan Page/British Institute of Management, London, 1988

Zimmer, Marc, *A-Z of Small Business Finance*, Sphere Books, London, 1985

GENERAL BUSINESS READING

Brealey, Richard, and Myers, Stewart, *Principles of Corporate Finance*, McGraw-Hill, (International Student Edition), various editions.

Handy, Charles B., *Understanding Organisations* (third edition), Penguin Books, London, 1985

Peters, Thomas J., and Waterman, Robert H., *In Search of Excellence*, Harper and Row, New York, 1982

Slatter, Stuart, Corporate Recovery: *A Guide to Turnaround Management*, Penguin Books, London, 1984

GLOSSARY

Articles of Association: in conjunction with the Memorandum of Association (which deal with the external relationships of a company), these set out the objects of the company (usually defined very widely), its borrowing powers, directors' voting rights, the number of shares to be issued, etc. The Articles are a form of constitution for the company. Basic Articles and Memoranda can be acquired over the counter at law stationers.

asset base: this is the tangible assets that a company owns – buildings, equipment, stock, work in progress. Intangible assets – *goodwill*, brand names, etc. – are not included.

balance of payments deficit/surplus: where the value of imports, visible and invisible added together, exceeds the value of exports – generally the case in the UK. A surplus is the converse. (Visible trade is trade in goods, invisible in services.)

balance sheet: the listing of a company's assets versus its liabilities – these are always given as equal.

base rate: this is the rate set by the Bank of England at which it will lend to discount houses who in turn on-lend to banks.

bear/bull market: in a bear market the consensus is that the value of shares is on a downward trend. A bull market is where optimism prevails.

bear raids: this is where a number of companies collude to sell a company's stock, thus driving down the price. Often a tactic during takeovers to reduce a predator's strength.

BES: this stands for Business Expansion Scheme. These schemes were promoted by the government in the 1980s to encourage investment in new projects or enterprises. Investors in such schemes enjoyed a tax holiday on dividends and capital gains from their investments (basic rate only) so long as they left their money in the project for five years.

bonds: bonds are a form of IOU issued by companies or governments. They carry a fixed rate of interest (called the coupon as originally entitlement to interest was on a coupon attached to the bond) and must ultimately be repaid by the borrower, unlike *preference shares*.

branding its service: much effort is devoted to branding services in the hope that this will increase customer/consumer awareness of what a product or service is (e.g. Parcel Force, Inter-City, Dyno-Rod, First Direct).

brands: see *valuing brands* in the *balance sheet*.

bull market: see *bear market*.

cartel: this exists where a group of companies collude within a market to fix prices, quantity of product supplied, etc. Suspected or actual cartels over the years include the airlines, the banks and petrol companies.

conversion window: this is the period during which the right to convert from one form of holding (preference shares or debentures) to ordinary shares may be exercised.

convertible: this is either a debenture (long-term company *bond* – or loan stock) or a *preference* share to which are attached rights of conversion to ordinary shares after a certain period of time has elapsed.

convertible preference shares: see *convertible* and *preference* share.

coupons see *bonds*.

debentures: in the UK these are long-term bonds secured on fixed assets (in the US they are unsecured).

dilution: this is where the value of existing shares is lessened by a new issue; i.e. if 100 shares worth £1 currently exist and 20 new shares of 90p are issued (the price of shares in a rights issue or share offer is usually less than that at which current shares are listed to make them more attractive), then the value of the shares will be (£100+£18)/120 = 98.33p – all the shares are now diluted; furthermore, one's previous shareholding is diluted by virtue of the fact that it now only has 5/6 of its prior voting rights.

DTI: Department of Trade and Industry, responsible for fostering and overseeing private enterprise.

drafting: drawing up of documents. For a prospectus this can be a lengthy business due to the number of advisors involved and because it is critical that potential investors receive an accurate (and attractive) picture of the business.

earnings per share (EPS): these are the net profits (after tax) of a company divided by the number of shares in that company.

earn-out: buying a company on an earn-out basis means paying part of the purchase price at the time of purchase, the residue (or a proportion of it if the company does not meet an agreed earnings level) being paid at an agreed later date, which can be several years. Earn-outs protect the emptor from inadequate company performance and are frequently used when buying service companies which are hard to value (due to much of this value residing in 'goodwill').

EPS: see *earnings per share*.

equities: equity is the part of the company owned by the shareholders. Equities thus mean shares.

equity investor: a person or institution investing in shares rather than government *bonds* or *debentures*.

European Monetary System: this is a system aimed at achieving monetary integration within the EC. It recognises that the stability of exchange rates within the EC should aid long-term growth. Its main instrument is the *Exchange Rate Mechanism* (which the UK joined in 1990) with the ECU acting as reference currency.

Exchange Rate Mechanism: the ERM ensures that member states' currencies maintain closely regulated exchange rates, with fluctuation bands of 2.25% for the stronger currencies, and 6% for the weaker (including the pound and the lira). When a currency approaches the floor or ceiling of its fluctuation band, central banks intervene to restore the correct parity.

exit multiple: companies are often measured in terms of their *price/earnings ratio* or 'multiple'. When a business is taken over the price paid for the business is converted into the price per share which, divided by the *earnings per share*, gives a multiple. This becomes an exit multiple for the existing shareholders who are leaving the company by selling their shares in it.

flotation: this is the offering of shares for public sale. Companies must be plcs and usually launch themselves on the Unlisted Securities Market (USM). A high market flotation is one where shares are sold at a *premium*.

franchise: a system whereby the franchisor offers a ready-made business to the franchisee. The franchisee pays the franchisor to acquire the franchise. Generally the franchisor will provide support such as help in starting up, regional or national marketing and advertising, ongoing business advice and discounts on business requisites. Thus independent businesses, conforming to the requirements of the franchise, acquire the benefits of being part of a recognised chain and the necessary equipment for the business. The franchisor gains the dedication of the franchisee and expands at low cost.

FT Index/Dow Jones: the *Financial Times* Index lists virtually all shares regularly traded on the Stock Exchange. It is subdivided into the FT-30 and FT-100 indexes which list representative samples (in that they give a picture of general share performance) of companies. The Dow Jones is the US equivalent, based on the New York Stock Exchange.

full listing: this is achieved when a company moves from the USM to the Stock Exchange.

gearing: gearing refers to debt. A company's gearing ratio is the ratio of debt (i.e. loans from banks) to *equity*. The gearing position of a company refers to the status of this ratio.

go-go funds: these were funds that specialised in buying companies with undervalued property assets, which were then onsold at a profit.

gilts: these are government bonds, so called because the certificates were originally gilt-edged.

going public: the same as flotation.

goodwill: when one company takes over another, the difference between the price paid and the book value of the target company is known as goodwill. Under UK accountancy practice this is usually written off, effectively reducing the aggregate value of the two companies; this in turn means that the aggregate borrowing capacity of the combined or consolidated companies is reduced which makes the concept of goodwill unpopular with many companies. See also *valuing brands*.

high yield/risk: where an investment is considered more risky, investors require a greater return on their money. Exactly the same principle is applied to setting the odds at horse races.

income stream: this is the flow of cash into a business due to that business's main activity (rather than from interest it may earn on deposits or from ownership of shares in other companies).

indemnity terms: in the context of this book, these are the terms set by the brokers and underwriters in the case of a flotation, whereby the company agrees to refund the brokers or underwriters if a target selling price is not met, and they have sustained losses. Indemnities have also been offered in share-support schemes (e.g. in the Guinness takeover of Distillers) – such indemnities sail close to the wind.

institutional investors: the institutions are organisations such as banks, pension funds, insurance/assurance companies that deal in large blocks of shares to generate part of their income (they often also hold government stocks).

LAUTRO: Life Assurance and Unit Trust Regulatory Organisation, an SRO (self-regulatory organisation), set up after the Gower Report, to monitor the activities of life assurance and unit trust companies.

listing: to be listed on a stock exchange is to have one's shares traded in on that exchange. See *full listing* and *USM*. In the UK shares are 'traded' on the USM and 'listed' on the Stock Exchange.

long- and short-form reports: a long-form report is a full set of company accounts, including a profit and loss account, a balance sheet, sources and applications of funds and a full set of notes detailing the numbers included in the foregoing. A short-form report might just include a balance sheet and a profit and loss account, with very limited notes and without any breakdown by activity of a company's accounts. The long-form report is prepared for the sponsors of an issue so that they can evaluate the worth of any target company and require the rectification of any apparent problems within the target company. The short-form report appears in the share offer document, which a predator issues to raise money for the purchase.

MMC: the Mergers and Monopolies Commission. Takeovers and mergers are referred to the MMC if there is a fear that a monopoly or other market distortion will be created (a monopoly is generally considered to be a 25% share of any particular market).

nil net asset value: this means that a company's assets (buildings, equipment, stock, debtors, cash) are equal to its liabilities (creditors, dividends and tax). Assets can include *goodwill* and other intangibles, such as *brand* names, though including such items on the *balance sheet* is still controversial.

old money: in the sense used here it means capital locked up in a business, usually because shares in that business are not traded. This capital has been built up by investment in the business and by the growth of a business or simply by inflation causing a rise in value of the company. Old money is unlocked by selling the company, whereby the owners/shareholders receive cash for their interest.

ordinaries, ordinary shares: these are the standard type of share, with voting rights but no guarantee of a dividend.

organic growth: this is growth achieved by the success of a business in its activities as opposed to expansion by acquisition.

over-the-counter (OTC) market: this is a market for securities not listed on the Stock Exchange and which are traded, nationally and internationally, directly between buyers and sellers.

paper: a slang term for share certificates. A company can authorise and issue shares virtually at will (once necessary changes to the *Articles of Association* have been made), just as banks can print paper notes. Issuing paper means launching new shares, via a rights issue, on to the market. Expensive paper in this book refers to the high value attached to the shares of a company. When this is high it is possible to borrow more money against them as they are considered a form of security. Hence the term 'security' for shares.

placing agreement: this is the agreement between a company placing shares and its broker as to the terms on which the shares will be issued.

placing: this is an issue of shares through a rights issue. It often, too, refers more specifically to the selling by a broker direct to institutions, without a public issue.

plc, limited company: plc stands for public limited company; a company must be a plc before it can offer shares to the public. Unlike a 'private' limited company a plc can sell shares without reference to other shareholders (though see *rights issue*). A plc must have issued share capital of £50,000 of which £12,500 must be fully paid up. It must also submit full annual accounts to Companies House. 'Limiting' a company means that its shareholders are only liable for the nominal amount of the shares that they hold in the event of winding up or liquidation.

preference shares: these are 'preferred' in that payment of dividends on these shares occurs before payment of dividends on ordinary shares. Often they are 'cumulative', that is, where dividends are not paid in one year, they are carried forward to the next. The dividend on a preference share is fixed, i.e. it is effectively interest, as for a *bond*, and is hence sometimes loosely known as a coupon. Unlike bonds, preference shares do not require redemption. Frequently, though, they are *convertible*.

premium: in the context of a placement of shares this means the amount by which the market selling price exceeds that at which the share is offered for sale.

price/earnings ratio: this is the price of a share divided by the *earnings per share*.

profit and loss margins: profit margins are the positive difference between income and expenditure (loss margins the reverse). There are several sub-divisions: the 'gross' margin is the difference of sales minus direct cost of sales (a − b below). The 'operating' profit or margin is this profit after other expenses, e.g. office expenses, staff, bank charges and interest, have been deducted (a − b − c). The 'net' profit is that after tax.

Sales/turnover	a
Cost of sales	b
Gross margin	a − b
Operating costs	c
Operating profit	a − b − c
Tax	d
Net profit	a − b − c − d

Dividends are paid from net profits.

proforma balance sheet: this is a balance sheet prepared for the formalities when going public or when arranging loans with a bank. Balance sheets are normally prepared as part of the annual accounts, but proformas are prepared at any time for the above purposes.

prospectus: the document that describes a company before it is launched on the USM or Stock Exchange to potential shareholders. It usually sets out the company's activities, its aims, who the directors are, gives some historical financial information and informs readers of the price at which shares will be issued and where they may be applied for.

public institutions: this means publicly quoted institutions (i.e. institutional investors) in the context of this book.

Restrictive Practices Act: the purpose of this Act is to eradicate practices that reduce competition or distort competition. For example, trade union demarcations were considered restrictive; more recently attention has focussed on the professions, law for example, where solicitors have to be represented in court by barristers and where solicitors had a monopoly on conveyancing. Fixed minimum commissions charged by brokers were also considered restrictive.

retainer: an amount paid, usually on an annual basis, so as to have the services of particular advisors on call.

rights issue: a rights issue precedes a new share issue. All existing shareholders must have the right to buy all of any new shares issued, so as to be able to retain their degree of control over a company. These rights are often sold on to others who may wish to buy the shares or are traded in their own right.

selling 'off the page': this means to sell by advertising in magazines or periodicals – as opposed to other means of selling: via sales representatives, direct mail, retail, etc. – giving a contact address or phone number.

short-term EPS: the earnings per share over the short term. In general, the City looks to short-term EPS as it is interested in quick returns on its money rather than long-term growth and increase in capital value.

short-form report: see *long-form* report.

stay of execution: deferring the date by which an obligation, such as paying off a debt, must be performed.

takeover panel: this is an organ of the Stock Exchange responsible for ensuring that companies comply with Stock Exchange rules during takeovers and mergers.

underwriter: usually a bank, the underwriter agrees to buy in a company's shares when they are issued if the market fails to subscribe at the launch price. A fee is charged for underwriting.

USM/Unlisted Securities Market: the purpose of the USM is to provide a means whereby companies can raise cash through the selling of shares to the public. A company has to trade successfully on the USM before it can become fully listed. A company need place only 10% of its equity on the USM (25% for a full listing on the Stock Exchange) and is eligible with a shorter trading history, requiring only 3 years of audited accounts.

valuing brands: this is a relatively recent phenomenon, whereby companies try to increase the value of their assets by giving notional values to their brand names. This enables them to increase their liabilities, i.e. long-term creditors (loans) and shareholders' funds. It is controversial because brand value cannot be accurately quantified; it also effectively makes a nonsense of the 'good accountancy' practice of writing off *goodwill*.

venture capital: this is capital provided to help launch new businesses or to help small businesses to buy other companies or launch new projects. Because such ventures tend to be risky, it is usually quite expensive in terms of interest rates and other conditions. For example, *convertible preference shares* are often part of the package.

INDEX